Henry Brainard Kent

Graphic Sketches of the West

Henry Brainard Kent

Graphic Sketches of the West

ISBN/EAN: 9783337014681

Printed in Europe, USA, Canada, Australia, Japan

Cover: Foto ©ninafisch / pixelio.de

More available books at **www.hansebooks.com**

GRAPHIC SKETCHES

OF

THE WEST

BY

HENRY BRAINARD KENT.

CHICAGO
R. R. DONNELLEY & SONS, PUBLISHERS
1890

To
MY GENIAL COMPANION IN TRAVEL,
ELWIN R. KENT, ESQ.,
(" THE SECRETARY ")
THESE PAGES ARE FRATERNALLY INSCRIBED.

CONTENTS.

CHAPTER I.
FLIGHT TO TROPICAL CLIMES.

Taking Leave of Boreas. — "In Search of Winter Sun-beams." Scenes and Incidents along the Route. — The International Hopper. — Mischief of a Mountain Fairy. — New Mexico. — The Pacific Coast. — Solid Comfort 15

CHAPTER II.
SOUTHERN CALIFORNIA.

Los Angeles, — Eastern People Seeking a Sanitarium. — Booms in Real Estate. — How the Newcomer is Entertained 28

CHAPTER III.
IN PURSUIT OF GAME.

Operating in Jack Rabbits. — The Secretary and his Wild Meat Enterprise — Amateur Sporting League. — The Degenerate Jack. — Wild Game of the Pacific Slope 44

CHAPTER IV.
CLIMBING THE SIERRA MADRES.

A Feat of Pedestrianism. — Ascent to the Top of Mount Wilson. — Half-Way House. — A Treacherous Spot in the Trail. — Other Perplexities. — Overcoming Snow-bound Steeps. — Panorama From the Summit. — A Novel Ride................ 61

CHAPTER V.
RAMBLES BY RAIL.

San Gabriel — Ontario. — San Bernardino. — Riverside. — Principal Towns on the Coast. — Peculiar Flora of the Coast Range. — Retrospect... 75

CONTENTS.

CHAPTER VI.

INTO THE HEART OF THE SIERRAS.

The Ride Through the San Joaquin. — A German Financier and Government Prices. — Gold Mines, Deer, Pigeons and Quails. — "Big Tree" Station. — The Summit. — Inspiration Peak.. 87

CHAPTER VII.

EARTH'S CROWNING GLORY.

A Fairyland of Picturesque Scenes in the Yosemite — El Capitan and His Battalion of Boulders and Monoliths. — Rides and Rambles About the Valley. — Tracing Cañons. — Imposing Cataracts. — Inspiring Peaks. — Dizzy Heights. — Kaleidoscopic Scenes. — Never-ending Beauties 101

CHAPTER VIII.

THE MAMMOTH TREES.

The Mariposa and Calaveras Groves. — Vegetable Curiosities. — "Grizzly Giant." — "Wawona." — Other Celebrities and Other Prolific Species of the Sierras. — The Fifty Mile Flume. 120

CHAPTER IX.

OBJECTS OF INTEREST IN THE GOLDEN STATE.

San Francisco and Its Superb Hotels. — Golden Gate Park. — Cliff House. — Chinatown. — San Francisco to Mount Shasta. — Lake County. — The Geysers. — Petrified Forest. — Wild Mountain Staging. — Blue Lakes. — Saratoga Springs. — Recreations 134

CHAPTER X.

THE CLIMATE OF CALIFORNIA.

Local and Other Opinions. — Theory of Uniform Temperature. — A Fine Winter Resort. — The Warmer Months. — Heat of the Interior Valleys. — The Coast. — Northern California. — Its Foot Hills and Mountain Retreats. — Thermal Belt. — Precaution 149

CHAPTER XI.

THE CITY OF THE SAINTS.

Leaving the " Golden State." — Crossing the Sierras. — The Desert Ride. — Salt Lake City and Its Picturesque Environments. — Features of Interest. — Temple Block. — Strange Institutions. — A Noted Mormon Avenue. — The City and Its People. — A Boy's Opinion of His Grandfather 167

CHAPTER XII.

IN PURSUIT OF KNOWLEDGE.

Indoor and Outdoor Mormonism. — The Soul of the System. — The Communicative Saint Who Had Traveled a Long Road. — Mormonism the Exponent of all Wisdom. — Plural Marriage. — The Second Revelation Knocks Out the First. — Whatever the Church Says is Right. — Development of the Gods....... 186

CHAPTER XIII.

STATEHOOD FOR UTAH.

Sudden Stampede of the Saints. — "The Peoples' Party" and Their Bid to the Gentiles. — The Proposed Constitution. — Fine Diplomatic Distinctions. — Vital Parts of Mormonism. — Trap Doors. — Monogamists. — Martyrs. — Make up of Mormondom 204

CHAPTER XIV.

FROM THE JORDAN TO THE UNCOMPAHGRE.

Utah Valley. — Over the Wasatch. — Wonders of the Price River. — Castle Gate and Cañon. — Rock-hewn Battlements. — Nature's Architecture. — Castle of Torquilston and Its Strange Occupants. — The Uncompahgre Valley........................ 223

CHAPTER XV.

OVER THE ROCKIES. — MONTROSE TO MANITOU.

Cimarron. — Black Cañon of the Gunnison. — Its Distinctive Features. — Chippeta Falls. — Currecanti Needle. — Climbing the Steeps. — Among the Clouds. — Marshall Pass. -- Grand Cañon of the Arkansas. — The Royal Gorge. — Whither are We Bound? — Tartarus or Elysium? — Pike's Peak, Manitou and Garden of the Gods............................... 233

LIST OF ILLUSTRATIONS.

	PAGE.
Scenes in the Golden State,	14
Starting for the Tropics,	17
A Cañon of the Gallinas,	21
Pueblo Indians, New Mexico,	23
Giant Cactus of Arizona,	24
Starting for the Cañons,	25
Southern California Orange Orchard,	31
Presenting His Cause,	35
Scenes in the San Gabriel Valley,	41
To Be Handled With Care,	47
Mistaking His Intent,	51
Irreclaimable,	55
California Vulture,	59
A Refreshing Stream,	64
Cascade in the Sierra Madres,	68
The Last Pull,	70
Southern California Panorama,	72
View in San Antonio Cañon, Ontario, Cal.,	76
Inside and Outside Headers,	78
Santa Barbara Mission,	80
View From Castle Rock, near Santa Barbara,	82
Scene in the Coast Range,	84
Tropical Luxuriance, Del Monte,	86
The Loop,	89
The Flume,	92
A Cascade in the Sierras,	93
Summits of the Sierra Nevadas,	95
Entrance to Yosemite Valley,	98
Yosemite in Early Times,	103
Bridal Veil Fall,	105
Cathedral Rocks,	106
The Sentinel,	107
Yosemite Falls,	109

LIST OF ILLUSTRATIONS.

	PAGE
Mirror Lake,	111
North Dome,	112
South Dome,	113
Views in the Valley,	115
Falls of the Yosemite,	117
Among the Pines of the Sierras,	119
Measuring the Grizzly Giant,	121
The Wawona,	123
Hollow Trunk,	125
Keystone State,	127
In the High Sierras,	129
On the Coast,	131
Cliff House,	133
On Wheels, Through Golden Gate Park,	135
Alley, Chinese Quarters,	137
San Francisco Bay,	139
Vulcan's Steam Works,	141
The Petrified Forest,	143
The Devil's Cañon.	145
Rough but Romantic,	147
Fruit Scene in Southern California,	151
Tropic Foliage, Coast,	153
Residence Montecito, Coast,	155
Woodard's Gardens, Golden Gate,	157
Napa Soda Springs, Orange and Vine Culture,	161
Fruit Ranches, Northern California,	163
Haunts of the Trout,	167
The State Capitol,	171
Over the Sierra Summits,	173
Lake Esther, Sierra Nevada Mountains,	175
Lake Donner,	177
Lake Tahoe,	179
Scenes in the Nevada Desert,	181
"Hostile Elements,"	183
Bird's-Eye View of Salt Lake City,	189
Seeking Information,	191
The Temple,	195
The Tabernacle,	197
Bee Hive House,	199
The Great Salt Lake,	201

LIST OF ILLUSTRATIONS.

	PAGE.
Eagle Gate,	205
Amelia Palace,	207
Lion's Head Rock, Great Salt Lake,	209
Tramway in Little Cottonwood Cañon,	211
Weber Cañon,	215
Echo Cañon,	217
A Romantic Retreat, American Fork Cañon,	219
Castle Gate,	225
Uncompahgre River,	227
On the Reservation,	229
Approach to the Black Cañon,	235
In the Black Cañon,	237
Currecanti Needle,	239
Marshall Pass,	241
Royal Gorge,	243
A Refreshing Spring, Cascade Cañon,	244
A Cool Retreat, Cascade Cañon,	245
Queen of the Cañons,	246
The Balanced Rock,	247
Manitou and Pike's Peak,	249
Rock Formations, Garden of the Gods,	251
Gateway to the Garden of the Gods,	253

PREFACE.

The contents of "Graphic Sketches of the West" are made up of selected portions of the writer's correspondence, recently published in two leading New York newspapers, and special articles and additions written for the express purposes of the book.

Its presence on the market in this form is largely due to the encouragement which the published portions have already received from the press and the public, having been not only widely quoted, but also the subject of many pleasant allusions, to which the author's attention has often been kindly directed by the editors and their associates. The latter have also suggested the title which the book bears.

It is, perhaps, pertinent to apprize the reader that this volume is not intended as a guide in the extreme sense. As such, it is feared that it might guide the tourist into some of the undesirable complications and indescribable embarrassments which the writer has experienced, and which he could not cheerfully recommend to the traveling public. But, in a more practical sense, it is believed that it will serve as a *general* guide to the country described, since it either gives detailed descriptions or makes brief mention of the principal objects of interest on the Pacific coast and the leading attractions of transcontinental routes. All details of small towns and cumbrous statistics, however, have been carefully avoided, that greater prominence might be given the more unique manifestations of life and character, and, especially, the eccentric and noteworthy exhibitions of nature.

The articles have been written as prompted by the suggestiveness of the subject in hand, entirely independent of corporate interests, and with appreciative readers always in mind. It is, therefore, hoped they will be cheerfully welcomed by such as maintain lively interest in the amenities of travel, at the same time serve practical purposes to the tourist and health-seeker, and in general both inform and please.

SCENES IN THE GOLDEN STATE

CHAPTER I.

FLIGHT TO TROPICAL CLIMES.

The tourist who visits Southern California in midwinter undergoes a metamorphosis hard to explain. People often wonder how it comes about that the grum and cantankerous habitant of the north is transformed into the cymophanous and agreeable bird that he is after reaching this country. The transition however, though complex and peculiar, is not entirely beyond the student of morphology. The writer, after much laborious investigation, has succeeded in eliciting facts and phenomena which ought to throw some light on this abstruse and hitherto unexplored field of research.

Beginning with the first stages of the transformation, the subject wakes up some frosty morning on the shores of the northern lakes and finds that, by some inadvertence, his room had not been hermetically sealed when he retired. The cold, piercing wind, charged with the terror of the lakes, lays siege to his slumbers, plays with his auburn locks, and by the break of dawn provides him with a swollen head and a new vocabulary. Bounding from his crib, he brushes about the room and summarily exhausts all the resources at his command for raising the temperature. Failing in this, he vainly tries, by both bell and yell, to raise the porter, and then sets about to raise Cain generally, and succeeds. Hastily pulling on his clothes, with one end of his collar buttoned to his vest, he rushes down to the office, peals off a volley of instructive epithets to the landlord, exhausts Crabb's Book of Synonyms in cursing the house, and vociferously declares his intention to skip the country and drown his troubles in the balm and sunshine of tropical skies.

Proceeding to put his resolve into execution, he takes the first train for Chicago, en route for the semi-tropics. On the journey he now and then opens the double-breasted car windows, humanely provided by large-hearted railroad managers, only to find that no change in the temperature is to be felt within telephone distance of the lakes. Perhaps at Chicago he may make life tolerable for a day or two within closed doors, especially if, as in the case of the writer, he enjoys the hospitality of one hundred and eighty test city cousins. But life loses its fascination the moment he steps out into the street, while a half-mile ride in a Chicago open "grip" (called by citizens "the refrigerator,") makes life no longer worth living for the time being. The next step is to call down the blessings of Olympus upon the heads of the convivial friends who have made your advent to the "Garden City" (not in winter) a festal occasion. Next after this is to call up the curses of Acheron against the hyperborean blizzards that patrol up and down the northern

FLIGHT TO TROPICAL CLIMES. 17

STARTING FOR THE TROPICS.

lakes without salary, and then push southward by fast express.

From Chicago to Kansas City the aggrieved fugitive from northern blasts, while enjoying the comforts of easy reclining chairs, elegant dining cars, the delicacies of the season, a good night's rest and moderating temperature, also gradually modifies his pessimistic views of life. As morning breaks upon his bewildered eye-balls, the first promise of endurable existence breaks upon his soul, and a thrill of ecstacy takes him in the back as he contemplates the practicability of crossing the platform to the dining car without congealing his marrow. Shortly he reaches Kansas City and is unceremoniously ushered into one of the greatest hippodromes on the continent—the Kansas City Union Depot. Here drummer, tourist, merchant, farmer, Negro, Chinaman, Jap, emigrant, millionaire —the elite, riff-raff and tag-rag of creation are all shoveled in together from the four quarters of the globe. Out-going trains make a daily sweep of this mixed population, only to make room for other in-coming hordes of equally interesting yet new specimens of creative genius. From this romantic city, situated on bluffs overlooking the Missouri river and its bordering prairies, the slowly evolving Californian pushes west and south by the Atchison, Topeka & Santa Fé railroad. For hundreds of miles he rides through prolific fields of vast extent, where standing stalks display an extravagance of growth that makes him more or less chagrined to think that he once tried to get rich raising corn on eastern city lots. In like manner the vast herds of cattle, roaming over the prairies bordering the Arkansas, bring up these same emotions when he recalls his late efforts in the east to build up a flourishing live stock business on one head of cattle and a quarter interest in the neighborhood pig. But this has nothing to do with the climatic features of the journey, except indirectly.

But lo! as we enter Colorado, the snowy summits of the Rockies appear, dazzling in the sunlight, ninety miles away, and soon the white Spanish Peaks loom upward in the distant sky. Reaching their base, we proceed to "surmount the rocky steeps." Up! up! one hundred and eighty five feet to the mile, we soon reach a land of frost and snow, still climbing until, six thousand feet in air, we are landed in the city of the Trinity — called Trinidad — the name, by the way, forming the principal religious association of the place. On entering this city it is with some difficulty that the tourist dispels the misleading impression that he is on his way back to Chicago, so visible are the signs of returning winter. While coming up this grade to Trinidad, occurs a little incident that may have an important bearing upon the tourist's future career in life. At a small way station near the base of the mountains a young damsel with roseate cheeks and luxuriant tresses enters the car in which you are seated. Her radiant eyes and erubescent lips captivate the beholder at first sight. All thoughts and higher ambitions are at once banished and bartered for the seemingly laudable desire of sharing the same seat, or at least entering into agreeable conversation with this bewitching fairy of the mountains. She appears to be acquainted with all the local passengers, talks with the seedy swain and lavishes her ravishing smiles upon the hoary-headed patriarch who hobbles about upon an antediluvian crutch; but not a word, nor a smile, nor a look of recognition has she for the worthy and blameless youth who so covets her addresses. It is of no avail to offer her the morning paper, knock an umbrella out of her hand by accident and humbly beg pardon— or even to inveigle an old fat man into her momentarily vacated seat and then graciously offer her ladyship a half interest in your own. Every strategem fails, and finally the rebuffed and discomfited youth strives to forget his defeats and disappointments by writing up his long neglected diary. After writing for half an hour with dynamical earnestness and seven-league-boot speed he begins to sneeze, wheeze, cough, snuffle and whoop. Casting a nervous glance to the rear, he discovers to his astonishment that this fair "Flower of Paradise," that deigned not to favor him with so much as a leer from her blooming and bewitching countenance, had seen fit to raise the window at his back and let in upon his defenceless head the unpropitious atmosphere of this mountain region. The cold which he contracts on this occasion is warranted to remain in *statu quo* after the usual administrations of hot punch and whisky sling, stand bullet-proof against compound oxygen, successfully resist all the medicinal virtues of New Mexico's boasted climate, and at the end of fourteen days show no more signs of being reduced than the price of board.

>Beware of Circe's cunning arts
>And the winsome maid of Trinidad,
>Leucosia's tongue, the queen of hearts,
>A draught at the back
>And a fearful cold in the head.

A CANON OF THE GALLINAS.

Stopping over one day at Trinidad to get a little initiated into Mexican life, introductory to the bigger dose to be taken further on, the climate-seeker again boards the train and pushes still on and up until he reaches the Raton Pass, which he enters in the snowy Colorado heights and from which he emerges into the sunny land of New Mexico. In going up this precipitous height to the pass, the train is divided into two sections to make sure that the iron horses (at least two to a train) will be equal to the ascent. By mistake the representative tourist boards the first section that comes along, and rides up the incline in a mysterious car that quite staggers his sensibilities. Its inmates seem to be contentedly employed in the various arts and industries, cooking beefsteak, washing dishes, mopping, "getting out washings" (in which latter occupation the washerwoman utilizes the bell rope for a clothes-line), and other domestic duties, all in harmonious operation. Having inquired of the conductor if the laundry and restaurant connected with the car are first class, and not being given the fullest assurance that they are, the luckless passenger, satisfied that he has "taken the wrong berth," disembarks at Raton. Here he transfers himself and effects to the second section, that has now pulled up to the summit.

From Raton the descent is made with such rapidity as to cause a depressing sensation on the ear-drum, similar to that experienced in descending a coal mine. Having passed the extensive cattle ranches of Dorsey and Ingersoll and the historic Wagon Mound, the rambler arrives at Las Vegas and its famous hot springs. Here he will be informed that an English gentleman, but a short time since, shot himself because he could not pay his bill at the Phoenix. Whereupon the listener is expected to make the following remark: "I would sooner think of shooting myself because I have to pay my bills." Then, after looking around to

PUEBLO INDIANS, NEW MEXICO.

see if any one has wit enough to see what a tremendous joke has been elaborated, he is ready to sample the cuisine of the institution. After taking one meal at this palace of luxury, built by railroad enterprise, he no longer wonders that a sensitive nature should have a feeling of delicacy about going off without paying his bill. This is a good place to feed an ordinary cold, and would doubtless put to rout almost any variety except that contracted while ascending the Trinidad heights. A fortnight's sojourn in this vicinity is most amusing and interesting. It affords the tourist an excellent opportunity to observe the peculiarities of the

GIANT CACTUS OF ARIZONA.
(Sixty feet high.)

Mexican "burro," (a demure, philosophical and recalcitrant variety of mule,) study the various forms and configurations of the ubiquitous "adobe" and various other phenomena, either ancient or odd, or both. The Mexican hasn't yet forsaken his wooden plow, carries stove-wood to market on horseback, and positively refuses to advance with the times.

STARTING FOR THE CAÑONS.

A most delightful ramble from the Phoenix Hotel is that up the river and cañons of the Gallinas. In these retreats of the mountains, nature poses in some of her loveliest attitudes, and few places will be found more picturesque and pleasing.

The tourist who is abroad for the purpose of sight-seeing, will not forget to stop off at Santa Fé—at least if interested in the antiquities and historical associations of the country. While here he will find it equally worth his pains to visit the mysterious relics of the far past, to be found at Embudo and other places a few miles north on the Denver and Rio Grande.

Leaving Santa Fé and casting a long, lingering, puzzled look back upon the long-headed "burro" and the short-waisted adobe hut, the pilgrim, destined to the land of sunny skies, passes through vast mountain regions, rich in mineral ores, over brick-colored lands, endless cactus fields, alkali lakes and desert wastes, and after a three days' ride, pulls up on the Pacific Coast, wondering if he is the same fellow that kicked up such a row at a certain eastern hotel because the climate wasn't half cooked. These are substantially the experiences of the reader's humble servant and the same programme is said to be in vogue for all making the trip under precisely the same circumstances.

The country over on this side of Uncle Sam's dominion is really *sui generis*. Warm breezes and cloudless skies, are served upon nature's lunch counter and at greatly reduced rates. Orange trees blossom, bud and bear, all at the same time; ripe tomatoes and real estate agents hang on all the year round, and the elements generally conspire to keep the muscles of the body and the buttons of the coat in a state of agreeable relaxation. People of the North, shivering in their overcoats, look with distrust upon all midwinter allusions to sultry skies, blooming flowers and ripening fruits. They are not however, poetic effusions, but, on the contrary, real, unvarnished and unsophisticated truths. The writer receives, almost daily, letters from the East, calling him an unconditional hypocrite and Janus-headed wolf in sheep's hide for sending these weather reports home to his friends. But I repeat they are mathematical verities and hold myself responsible for any mischief or inconvenience they may cause such as receive them without cavil or suspicion. The medicinal virtues of this country are beyond dispute. I have myself received more benefit here in one afternoon reading Buck Fanshaw and the binomial theorem than in cursing climate in the North for a whole winter.

CHAPTER II.

SOUTHERN CALIFORNIA.

THE people who have always lived in the staid East have but faint conception of the significance of the word "boom"—especially in the sense in which it has been illustrated in this locality. The cause of this is probably the great influx of Eastern people who have learned of Southern California as a sanitarium. In 1880, the population of Los Angeles was only eleven thousand. Now it is about fifty thousand. In December, 1886, four thousand tourists from the East came to this city during one week. Some idea of the Southern California boom may be conceived from the fact that in the year just mentioned thirteen thousand conveyances of real estate were made and twenty eight million dollars changed hands in Los Angeles county alone. This was nearly three times that of the preceding year, and though the ball still rolls, the prices are less fantastic and confounding. The old-time furor of '48 has never been fairly uprooted from California soil. This mania for rampant speculation seems to have become dovetailed into all the thoughts and sentiments of society. As inoffensive as the writer has always been reputed, it has been lively work for him to resist the elements of the all-pervading craze.

Upon reaching this county, about the first thing after making a few side trips to make sure of my whereabouts, was to make for an orange orchard. A large black dog made for me — I made for the fence. The owner suddenly made his appearance and requested me to explain. I was somewhat out of breath, but managed to collect my wind and wits, and replied: "Sir, I want to buy a good dog, and, seeing this one, I hooked the peroration of my coat into his bicuspids and walked off to see how hard he could pull."

"Well, I'll sell him to you — will sell anything, in fact — how does he suit? Does he pull satisfactorily?"

After bantering awhile and concluding the dog wasn't of the right color, I pushed on to the next fruit ranch, where there were no dogs for sale, and the owner of the ranch was totally blind. But this is a strange country, and notwithstanding the eternal darkness that clouded his brow, the old farmer approached and remarked:

"I am glad to see you. Where are you from?"

"The East, sir," I replied.

"Indeed!" continued the voluble gray-beard, "I was once an Easterner myself, but I have been here long enough to get my eyes opened."

"What! will this climate cure blindness? I have heard it was good for the wind, but this is something new you are telling me."

"No, *climate* can't do it, but real estate agents *can*. These fellows can open the eyes of an amblyopsis and make a man see stars with his collar bone."

"Aha! you seem to be up in science a little."

"Yes, I went to college in my younger days, but education is no protection to a man here when he is dealing with real estate agents. Nine-tenths of all the people who come here from the East have amaurosis of the eye-balls. They can't see with their eyes wide open half as much as a blind man with his eye-teeth cut."

"Now, Professor, I came here to buy a few oranges to eat, but I am greatly interested in this real estate business and want to learn all I can about it. I have heard it talked about ever since, and, for that matter, before, I left New York, and now that I am here I don't hear anything else."

"Well, I can tell you all there is to it in very few words. Did you notice that fruit ranch about eighty rods below here as you came along?"

"Yes, sir. I called there a few minutes ago to see about buying a dog."

"Did you notice what a fine place it was?"

"Yes, sir, on approaching it; but when I came away I was in somewhat of a hurry and didn't look around much."

"Well, what should you say that small twenty by thirty house and those twenty acres of land ought to be worth?"

"O! say one hundred and twenty-five dollars per acre."

SOUTHERN CALIFORNIA ORANGE ORCHARD.

"Well," continued the reverend gaffer, "that's about all it's worth, but three years ago it sold at one thousand five hundred dollars per acre."

"G-r-e-a-t Scotland! Why! you can buy city lots East for that price. Was it really worth it at that time?"

"No; but it sold for that."

"To whom?"

"Some Eastern chap paid that for it—"

"But Yankees don't generally pay for more than they get?" I interrupted.

"So it is in this case. I see you look puzzled, but I'll explain. Now look me square in the eye and I'll elucidate." (Somehow I couldn't get track of the old man's eye, but he proceeded:)

"Now it's on this wise. You fellows from the East come out here with a busted lung, the back-ache, or some malady of some sort that's got into the family, and before you are fairly planted on the platform here, you are spotted by a real estate agent. In a day or two you are seen driving around the country with him. As you take in the air and discover it to be an improvement on that which you left in the smoker, you are informed with much glow of sentiment that this is the only country the Almighty ever intended man should inhabit. Well, to cut the matter short, in less than three days, you are in possession of papers conveying clear title to twenty-five or fifty feet front of this California climate—the same to extend backwards one hundred feet, and upwards to the seventh heaven —to have and to hold henceforth eternally and forever.

Thousands of Eastern people come to this valley every season, and not a small per cent. of them are 'brayed in the mortar.' No wonder land has been high."

"Then you think people from the East don't get their money's worth here?"

"O, they get what they pay for. The man who buys this ranch where you say you went to buy a dog, pays about two hundred and fifty dollars per acre for the land, one hundred and fifty dollars for irrigating privileges, and the remaining eleven hundred dollars per acre for climate, gush, livery bills, getting his eyes opened, and so forth."

"Now, sire, just what does a man pay for climate in the above transaction?"

"Well, 'sonny,' you've got me. This matter of climate is a variable factor and very hard to estimate. It depends largely on location. Fifty feet front of it in Los Angeles or Pasadena often brings as much as five or ten acres out here in the country. The same acreage of climate is worth more to one man than another also. Hence you see we can't just size up this climate business, exactly."

"But so long as Eastern people can sell what they buy for as much or more than they pay, they are not hoodwinked very much, are they?"

"Perhaps not, but some morning somebody wakes up and discovers that he can't realize on his investment. His neighbor and his neighbors' neighbor discover the same thing, and a new slate is made up."

"But isn't this one of the most charming valleys of California?"

"Yes, this is one of the eighty-seven most charming valleys of the State, and when the State becomes more fully developed they are all going to be stretched on the bed of Procrustes together—at least so far as the 'charming' business is concerned. They are all charming and one is about as much so as another—at least I can't tell any difference in them."

"Then you don't think these speculators will succeed in getting a corner in this climate?"

"Hardly. A State that is equal in size to all of New England, New York and New Jersey, with room enough left to fence in Switzerland and half a dozen States like Delaware, isn't going to be cornered right away."

"I know, Professor, but isn't there a good deal of waste land in the State?"

"There are one hundred million acres of land in California, and thirty million of these are capable of a high state of cultivation; and as far as climate is concerned, almost any of it is good enough for a king. No; these real estate operators can't get a corner in this country."

"Well, uncle, if I keep on asking questions, I'm afraid I'll talk the daylights out of you."

"I wish they might be talked into me; but you spoke about some oranges. Just come this way and I'll show you my Washington Navels."

With elated jowl and glowing palate I followed on in the footsteps of the venerable rustic as he led the way to a place where

* * * " The lemon and piercing lime,
With the deep orange glowing through the green,
Their lighter glories blend."

On the way the process of irrigating orange orchards was illustrated, the manner of storing the water in reservoirs in the mountains described, and the mysteries and methods of irrigation generally unfolded. It appears the water is owned by companies, who sell it to the ranchmen at so much per share.

After sampling some fine navel oranges, some of which were a foot in circumference and of unexcelled flavor, I duly acknowledged the hospitality of my curious host, and departed with distended pockets and swelling emotions. Before reaching town, however, I had a slight set-back, being encountered by a number of plausible chaps, who were very desirous to show me where I could make a rap and scoop in a thousand dollars in less than two months without lifting a shovel.

There are several hundred real estate agents in and around Los Angeles. They are not only numerous, but also persuasive, plausible and hard to dodge. Worst of all, you may as well try to persuade the moon to irrigate the soil as to attempt to persuade these fellows that you are not out here to invest. You may point to your old clothes, turn your pockets wrong side out and swear by the precession of the equinoxes that there isn't a dollar in the whole macrocosm that you can call your own, and yet they persist until you are almost persuaded that you have something hid away somewhere that you had overlooked.

A few days ago there was an excursion to San

Diego in the interest of land owners. Your obedient servant was there. He had hardly struck Coronado Beach, however, when a *naive* land agent approached, with an oleaginous grin as broad as the smile of a beluga, and insisted in foreign accents upon selling a lot.

"No lots to-day, sir," I replied.

"To-morrow—you—buy—lot?"

"No, sir; haven't anything to invest."

"But—you—hav—*some*—monie," continued the pressing foreigner in measured syllables, "an'—when—you—see—ze—lot,—you—buy."

"No, sir, I haven't money enough to live decent. See what old clothes I wear."

"Oh, zat be comeek; ze cloze all right; where you stop?"

"Over at the New Carlton, but I haven't paid my bill yet."

"Oh! oh! ze hotel all right, ze cloze all right, ze monie all right; you buy one lot, you like it—fine! splendeed!"

"How much do you ask for your lots, anyway?"

"Moseer—genteelmo', I sell you one large lot for seven hundred dollars."

"Will you trust? How many onions can I raise off from it?"

"Onions? Oh! You raise no onions—"

"But if I buy the lot I should want to go to work on it and get a living. Couldn't I settle down to hard labor, go without pie, and in a few years pay for it by raising hogs or something of that sort? How

PRESENTING HIS CAUSE

large is the lot anyway — all I see here, probably — the whole island, isn't it?"

"Lor'-heving! No, no, no! Fourteen hundred lots here. You have twenty-five feet front for seven hundred dollar, an' you keep it two year an' you sell him fer two thousand dollar."

"Well! if that's so, I'll buy the lot."

"All right, moseer, I come to ze hotel to-morra, an' we go an' see ze lot, an' I sell him cheap, an' you make lot monie, ain't it?"

"Well, I'll see you round here to-morrow, perhaps."

"No, no, no. I go to ze hotel an' fine you, moseer, an' we come over togezer — ain't it?"

"No, you better not go there; you might not find me."

"Yes! yes! I be zair. I fine you. I sell ze lot cheap, you make monie, you get rich quick — don't it?"

They say, "there's a tide in the affairs of men, which, taken at the flood, leads on to fortune," but the next day I happened to be two hundred miles away and consequently out one thousand three hundred dollars. I must confess, however, I prefer on the whole, the direct methods of the San Diegoan just described to the periphrastic ones adopted by the American agents. The latter give you more queen's English, but the arguments advanced are the same, and I imagine a buyer would feel that he were paying for less poetry in the former instance. A man who earns his money by the sweat of his brow can scarcely afford to pay five or ten hundred dollars extra for a piece of property just to hear about the Elysian fields and the gardens of the Hesperides. Sometimes an agent will work himself up to the following:

"This is the land where the lemon trees bloom,
Where the gold orange glows in the green thicket's gloom,
Where the wind ever soft from the blue heaven blows,
And groves are of myrtle and orange and rose."

When such an effusion as the above is let off during a sale it is estimated that the buyer pays at least a thousand dollars for the effusion. Now you see this is too much when the complete works of Goethe can be had for a dollar. People who come here to invest, should insist upon buying the land without the poetry. More land and less poetry is the great demand of the times.

Yesterday I stepped into a certain real estate office and enquired about the healthfulness of the San Gabriel Valley. Rising to his feet and suddenly warming up to the subject, the broker replied with much enthusiasm:

"There is not another place in Southern California so favored as this San Gabriel Valley. I have now a number of fine lots in that quarter on my list. I was up there only last week and I was simply astonished at the beauty and promise of this valley. You see the Sierra Madres (pointing to the map) here extend almost due east and west, thus averting all adverse influences from the north. The soil, too, is porous and warm, and the water comes direct from the mountains, pure and refreshing. The foot hills slope gently to the south; there are no fogs; the air is dry and bracing, and the whole valley is bathed in perpetual sunshine. There is not a brighter nor fairer place in the whole universe."

"Is that so ?"

"Yes, sir ; and no better soil can be found. The whole valley is in a high state of cultivation. The San Gabriel Valley railroad actually runs through miles of orange orchards. Here are hundreds, yes thousands, of acres of the choicest land on earth. For miles the dark, rich foliage of fruit-burdened trees, interspersed with thriving vineyards, form a continuous fruit paradise, only interrupted by lovely cottages, exquisite floral lawns and princely courts. There are miles of avenues lined with lime and cypress hedges, or bordered by the stately eucalyptus. This whole tract, clear up to Pasadena and beyond, is one vast garden of tropical beauty and luxuriance."

"Is that possible ?"

"Yes, sir ; and the very air is laden with the aroma of these fruitful orchards and blooming gardens, while exhilarating sea-breezes are wafted over these sunny slopes freighted with eternal life."

"I want to know !"

"Yes, sir; and think of the scenery ! If you want to see scenery unparalleled, just get on top of the Raymond and take in the country. On the north the hills rise one above another until, towering six or seven thousand feet, they form the massive Sierras with their pine-clad slopes and picturesque cañons. Higher and higher they rise until, merging into 'Old Baldy' and Grayback, they reach the dizzy heights of ten and twelve thousand feet and lose their hoary heads in Paradise."

"Is this all in the San Gabriel valley ?"

SCENES IN THE SAN GABRIEL VALLEY.

"Yes, sir; all in the San Gabriel valley, and the half has not been told at that. The scenery I spoke of is all on the north. In the opposite direction the San Clemente and Cataline islands rise up out of the ocean, standing bold and bare against the distant sky, and overlook the broad expanse of the Pacific like colossal giants — 'sentinels of the mighty deep.' Why? Bryant alluded to this valley when he spoke of —

> * * * * * * * " 'The hills,
> Rock-ribbed and ancient as the sun — the vales
> Stretching in pensive quietness between;
> * * * And poured round all,
> Old ocean's gray and melancholy waste.'

"I tell you a man can't live in this valley I am talking about without becoming a poet. These orchards of Hesperides, Elysian fields and Gardens of the Gods —

> " 'Where the gold orange glows in the green thicket's gloom —' "

"Hold on! stranger, hold on!" I interrupted, "every place I have been to yet on this coast I have been told is the place

> " 'Where the gold orange glows in the green thicket's gloom.'

Now, I want to know if the oranges do this all over this country, or have these other fellows been lying to me?"

My friend, I am intensely in earnest in this matter," rejoined the broker, "and if you want a lot in this San Gabriel Valley I will sell you one that you can double your money on in less than three months."

"Oh! I have no idea of buying a lot; all I cared to know about this valley for was, I sent my mother-in-law up there last week. I guess I'll send and have her come back. By the way, don't you know of some place around here that isn't quite so healthy — one, for instance, where an elderly lady with an extra allowance of vim and aggressiveness would find it 'nip and tuck' to pull through another winter?"

Hereupon the eloquent broker's larynx came to a dead set and both parties to a better understanding.

CHAPTER III.

IN PURSUIT OF GAME.

From the time the versatile Nimrod founded the Assyrian Empire and the reckless Esau bartered his birthright for a bowl of soup, hunting appears in history as the favorite diversion both of gods and men Whether this proclivity of the race be wisely or unwisely entertained is little to the purpose. There is a fascination about pursuing a timid quadruped through orchard and meadow to his home in the underbrush that is peculiar if not unaccountable. The tendency exists and the fascination is attested by the sporting public throughout the world. The man who recalcitrates upon being asked to bring in an armful of wood, cheerfully consents to ford rivers and climb mountains to bag a partridge that can be bought for a quarter. I have known men who could earn ten dollars per day in their profession to hunt coyotes and prairie dogs at less than ten cents per week. Confronted with such significant facts and phenomena as these, how useless it is to deny the love of adventure a place among the implanted principles, or moralize upon the folly of wasting golden opportunities of becoming President in the pursuit of quails and cotton-tails!

Actuated by this innate thirst for adventure common to the race, the writer, joined by the late private secretary of one of New York's leading public men, has been making periodic invasions among the wild animals of this country. Securing at the outset a Colt's lightning repeater and an approved breech-loading shot-gun, we prepared to entertain all comestible flesh with magnificent fireworks. Going to a real estate agent in Los Angeles, we diligently inquired for the hunting paradise of which we had read. In reply we were promptly informed of a place not far away where a novice in the business could sit on a stump and kill forty jack-rabbits an hour. At that time we were not very well read in the fine art of selling city lots ten miles out of town. Besides there is an ingenuous credulity about an amateur sport that drinks in with fabulous avidity any statement which tends to increase the stock of slaughterable fauna incident to a new locality. Hence the representations of the real estate agent were not questioned. Any way we could view the subject, this direction seemed to offer special inducements. For one like myself who had at that time a sort of leaning toward honor and future reward, there loomed up the gilded circumstance that jack-rabbit squelchers are more esteemed in this country than oak planters. Irving said: "He who plants an oak plants for posterity," but he ought to have added that he who kills a jack-rabbit blesses both present and future generations—and thus have made himself immortal. On the other hand the tourist, like my partner, who had been fed on jack-rabbits at 75 cents per meal at the railway eating stations this side of the Rockies, might well view the pursuit of these tender fibered rodents from a *pecuniary* standpoint. On the basis of seventy five cents a rabbit and forty rabbits an hour, the secretary saw money in the business. Deciding, therefore, to carry out the real estate agent's instructions, we secured a rig and started out for the proposed field of operation. In the way the monetary considerations of the enterprise evidently preyed upon the mind of my associate, for all at once, after a long and ominous silence, his countenance lighted up with the inspiration that heralds the solution of a momentous problem, and he observed:

"Do you know what you are about, comrade? We are approaching a region abounding in game. We are here on expense, and why waste our ammunition? Why not make our amusement a source of income? Now what I propose is this: Let us go to the various markets in the city and contract our game. It may not have occurred to you, chum, but there's money in this business, rightly conducted."

"But suppose we should make contracts and not be able to fill them," I replied.

"Not fill our contracts? Why! you blockhead, we don't need to take orders for more than we can supply. We know sure, from what the real estate man told us, that we can each kill forty rabbits an hour. If we are gone four hours, that will be one hundred and sixty rabbits apiece, or three hundred and twenty to deliver in all. Now I propose that we go back to the city markets and contract three hundred rabbits by sundown. That will give us twenty to fall through on, and if by any possible mischance we should not happen to get quite enough this forenoon we will run out a little while after dinner, near town, and make up the number."

"But," I interposed, "three hundred rabbits will be quite a load, and how are we going to handle them?"

Mamillaria Elephantidens.

Mamillaria Macromeris.   Echinocactus Orcutti.

TO BE HANDLED WITH CARE.

"Why! you addle-pated loon, can't you see beyond your eye-winkers? We shall have to go to the livery stable, of course, make arrangements for a rig, with high sideboards on a double wagon, and have them carried direct from the field to the market. An enterprise like this can't be carried on with wind. I expect there will be some outlay, but where we spend one dollar we'll make ten. It's a good thing to know something when a man is three thousand miles from home."

These observations being rather emphatic, and fearing my partner might get to being personal, I thought best not to press my objections. After spending some time in these deliberations, however, we found it was getting time to do something and so proceeded without returning to the city to make the proposed contracts. We concluded that we could this time pile our game in heaps and haul it to market in the afternoon.

Advancing along a broken wagon road through thickets of cactus, chamisal and greecewood, we succeeded at last in reaching the sportsman's paradise so big with promise — not, however, without encountering a number of difficulties in the way. One of these was a river, which at that time was swollen from melting snows on the mountains. In crossing this we performed several daring feats of equestrianism in which conveyance, steed and sports all barely escaped an aqueous inhumation. We now dismounted, tethered our beast and made for suitable stumps from which, as the base of our operations, we at once inaugurated hostilities with all marketable game — but especially the wily, mischief-making rodents that promised such flattering returns to both skill and labor. With eyes, ears and guns cocked, we boldly awaited our victims. Now and then a stray rabbit would leap out from the thicket and instantly disappear. We had confidently believed that we should make the surrounding country, for at least a radius of half a mile, an uninterrupted field of slaughter — a scene of carnage — an aceldama of broken bones, a sort of open-air packing house, from which cargoes of muscle-making pabulum would be shipped to the markets of the state. But

> " Oft expectation fails, and most oft there
> Where most it promises."
> " The sweets we wish for turn to loathed sours,
> Even in the moment we call them ours."

We watched and waited in good faith, but somehow the rabbits didn't live up to their appointments. Time flew rapidly on. The forenoon was fast wearing away; our forefingers were in suspense and our fore-tops in painful anxiety. The secretary, indeed, writhed in mortal restlessness; he couldn't understand the situation; his three hundred jack rabbits didn't show up — his estimates didn't realize. Changing tactics, repairing to other stumps, lying in ambush, skirmishing about in jungles and arroyos, were all in vain. At last, in our desperation, we threw up the white flag to these skulking denizens of the day and retreated from the field. I now had a pressing inspiration to call the attention of my comrade to the superior judgment which I had evinced in opposing heavy contracts on an uncertainty; but, by a strong effort of the will I controlled these impulses and repressed the inspiration. Events which followed proved my wisdom in so doing. For before sun-down my partner's feelings had reached a state of maturity, which, were it not for a timely interposition, would have culminated tragically. The circumstance is this : A friend of ours at the hotel, while talking to another about the school building at Los Angeles, inadvertently used the word "contract," in the course of his conversation. My partner did not seem to catch the connection, and proceeded at once to make a personal assault upon the supposed offender. With flushed face and jugular vein distended in rage, he throttled his undeserving victim and threatened his equilibrium before I had time to intercede ; nor did the disturbance entirely subside until I had carefully explained, and fully assured the secretary that the gentleman referred to a *building* contract, and was making no allusion whatever to our rabbit enterprise.

Right here, in justice to my partner, I will say, I have found him, on the whole, docile, good-humored and easily pleased. There appears, in fact, only this one subject upon which he seems to be especially sensitive, and I therefore respectfully caution the public against the danger of ever using, in his hearing, in any ambiguous or equivocal sense, the word *contract*. To be actually safe, better not use the word at all or *any* word that might be mistaken for it. For this reason the word *compact* is objectionable, and there is no absolute security except in the use of such terms as "covenant," "written or parol stipulation," "mutually-concurred-in arrangements," or something similar. The word *contract* is positively hazardous.

The following day we were joined in our recreations by two other would-be sports — the one a capitalist from Ohio, who is here speculating in real estate, the

IN PURSUIT OF GAME. 51

MISTAKING HIS INTENT.

other a Chicago commission merchant. These were very anxious to learn the use of fire-arms, and so we admitted them into our circle, which was thereupon designated the "Consolidated New York, Ohio and

Illinois Amateur Sporting Confederation." This name seemed to promise the institution a permanent existence ; but like others of its kind it proved short-lived — lasting indeed, but a single day. The circumstances which brought about its dissolution are of a peculiar character, and I hereby propose to fearlessly show up the inside history of this remarkable organization, which is briefly this :

The Ohio and Illinois members of the league, hob-nobbing with the " contract " division of its New York constituents (the secretary), secured a defunct jack rabbit (which they probably purchased at the market), and secretly tied him up to a short stake, in the same standing attitude which is assumed in the chase. They then succeeded, by a series of cunningly contrived expedients, in decoying your humble servant to the scene of action. The expression of ecstacy which came over my deluded physiognomy, as I beheld the alluring rodent, erect upon his haunches, challenging my skill, was, doubtless, ineffable. I fell to my knees to escape observation, took aim, and blazed away. The rabbit didn't move. Another bang, and the beast still stood erect. "I'll swallow my gun if that animal isn't deaf as a stone wall," I observed, and let fly another dose of civilization, but still he lived. "I'll either kill or wake up that totally depraved harlequin of impudence, if I fight it out on this line all summer," I continued, and crash went another cartridge. But the dumb beast still held his ground. Click! flash! clash! flew another slug. Volley after volley followed, but brazen-faced jack only stared with a sort of incorrigible grin, which said, "Crack away; I'm not afraid of your popgun." More and more incensed by this defiant attitude, I continued the fusilade, pouring the shrapnel into his obstinate head and stiff-necked back with unrelenting perseverance. But all efforts to reclaim the felonious offspring of shameless effrontery seemed in vain. Having now exhausted all my ammunition, I rushed upon my plucky antagonist and was about to break down his back with the stock of my gun, when I discovered that he was securely strapped to a stake. My chagrin was indeed beyond the power of computation, but I resolutely determined to maintain my dignity and keep my allies in blank ignorance of the antics which I had performed while being practiced upon by this reprehensible species of charlatanry. But what was my surprise, upon turning around, to discover my comrade, the Ohio capitalist and the Chicago boodler, gesticulating in the tall grass close by, in hilarious and jubilant convulsions. I should have, doubtless, opened fire upon them all had I not wasted my ammunition on the rabbit. As it was, being defenseless, while they were armed, I held my peace. My only redress seemed to be to withdraw from the order with which I had so unfortunately become associated. So I withdrew. The other members said they would like to withdraw also, and thereupon the C. N. Y. O. and I. A. S. C. was dissolved. But this did not completely solve the difficulty, for, when we reached the hotel, my hunting operations were carefully reviewed and publicly commented upon. Of course it didn't answer to show out any atrabilarious emotion in company, while to make a personal assault upon my defamers, after the manner of the secretary, was not in keeping with the moral character which I had thus far sustained. But if an unprincipled crew of scribes, land-sharks and boodlers ever again conspire to fraudulently inveigle me by another such imposture as this, neither decorum, reputation nor family antecedents will stay the hand of wrath or rob the scales of retributive justice. Those who sow the wind must expect to reap the whirlwind.

The following day was the Sabbath. Not feeling exactly comfortable at the hotel, and having a sort of secret premonition that something would be said in the sermon about jack-rabbits, I arose early and spent the day in deep meditation far up the Sawpit cañon of the Sierra Madres. In this remote fastness of the mountains I encountered a venomous rattlesnake. The fearful reptile gave the usual signal of danger by shaking his ill-boding rattles until the air was filled with an ominous whirr like that of swarming locusts. For a few seconds things were generally active. Two rifle-balls, one through the back and the other in the head, soon settled the question, however, and I passed on "like other conquerors, to muse upon the fearful ruin I had wrought."

Now I know that the veracity of this adventure will be questioned since there was no one along to witness the transaction. But I stand ready to swear by the perturbations of Jupiter, the sun's parallax and all the stars, clusters and nebulous aggregations that will parade the welkin for the next twelve months,

IRRECLAIMABLE.

that I did actually encounter, in mortal combat, just such a fateful monster in the ragged wilds of the Sierras. In addition to this sworn statement, I can show the rear appendage of the reptile in proof, and indeed did show it to my perfidious friends at the hotel.

They, as might be expected, contested my title to the distinction I claimed, and declared I had found the evidence of my alleged achievement somewhere in the way, or else bribed the dealer in curiosities to open his shop on Sunday. Now, I don't like to call on any more of the celestial luminaries, but if worst comes to worst, I will go on and summon the whole cosmogony to bear witness to the truth of this adventure. I have been argued out of several of my favorite adventures already, and am not going to be talked out of this one if I have to sit up nights to defend it.

Since coming to this country, many Eastern friends have made personal inquiries of me concerning the game to be found in Southern California. I meant to have got at this part of the subject before this, but the foregoing prelude seemed necessary to show up the impressive rites and ceremonies by which the novitiate is admitted into the mystic arcana of this exciting field of activity.

Besides the Eastern tourist himself, we have here in the way of game, notably the deer, jackass and cotton-tail rabbits, California plumed and mountain quails; and in the vicinity of the ocean and inland lakes, large quantities of geese and ducks. The larger game, such as the grizzly, black and cinnamon bear, formerly common in all the mountain ranges of California, are now so retired to the inaccessible portions of the Sierras that few efforts are made to hunt them out. In this southern region they are practically extinct. Not very long ago, however, a large grizzly was seen a few rods back of this hotel, walking off with a bee-hive under his arm toward the mountains. Mountain sheep or big-horn are getting very scarce, although it is rumored that a herd of considerable size rove about in the region of perpetual snow on the summit of "Old Baldy," one of the highest peaks of the Sierra Madres. Deer are occasionally taken in this part of the State, but more often further north. Occasionally the sportsman has the good fortune to find, in his wanderings, the locked antlers of the deer. These are considered nearly as great a triumph as to gather in the "bounding roebuck."

At certain seasons of the year the bucks engage in fearful combats, in which the horns spring and become inseparably interlaced. Once joined in this mysterious manner, the late bitter foes spend their remaining days in peace together — at least until one of them dies — when the other, gradually disenthralled from the spell which binds him to his mate in this strange alliance, shakes off the decomposing body of his partner and again is free. The antlers of his antagonist, however, are borne aloft, telling the tale of a battle both lost and won. An old hunter at this place gives an account of another curious phenomenon similar to this. A party of his acquaintance saw a buck bounding through the forest with a sort of globe attached to his antlers. Upon killing the animal the curious object proved to be a human skull — the remnant of a luckless adventurer who had fallen prey to one of his merciless blows.

Feathered game abounds in this region. When at San Diego I saw thousands of water birds, such as

Canada geese (called here honkers); speckled-breasted, white-billed, brown and China brants; mallard and canvas-back ducks, besides spoonbills, teals, blue-bills and red-heads in great number. As we passed Elsinore lake the shore was literally lined with this class of game. I have seen flocks of geese over a mile in length passing over this valley, preparing to make raids upon the wheat fields further north. The albatros, cormorant, pelican and sea-gull haunt the seashore.

But by far the most distinctively gamey of all California's fauna, worthy of the chase, is the plumed quail and the wily jack-rabbit. The California plumed quail is very plentiful in this country, and no fancy price is served up with quail on toast. Yet one needs to be alert to be successful in hunting the quail. These birds run along the ground inviting pursuit—seeming to know the exact range of your fowling piece. When this limit is reached they take to the air, and this is the time to take *them*—on the wing. The mountain quail is somewhat larger, but unsuspecting, and easily captured. I was once deluded into shooting one of these, supposing them to be like the rest of the quail tribe—able to take care of themselves.

Concerning the jack-rabbit there seems to be a prevailing misconception. Among unlettered races few have been more shamefully misrepresented. He is not the indiscreet, silly fellow supposed, and the sportsman who pursues him on regulation principles soon finds it out. Give him a respectable showing and he soon convinces you that he is anything but a *non compos mentis*. An animal that will run, dodge, walk on

CALIFORNIA VULTURE.
Next to the largest flying bird in the world,— four feet high, spread of wings ten to twelve feet,—nearly extinct.

tiptoes, crawl on his belly, skulk, hide, hobble as if wounded, and then, at a second's notice, shoot like a pencil of light across sward and fallow, is no freshman at the business. The most approved method of taking this game seems to be, as in hunting the quail, "on the fly," with a shot gun. The moment they appear, even if at considerable distance, is the appointed time. Once under headway they are lost and that without remedy. Shooting from the carriage is contrary to all ideas of decorum; for, becoming accustomed to the sight of moving vehicles, they continue to crop the cabbage leaf, gnaw the sapling or stare with indifference, and thus become an easy prey. The devout sportsman disdains to take any mean advantage of the unsuspecting rodent and no more thinks of firing upon him on such occasions, than he would think of dunning a friend at an evening party or firing on a flag of truce. Honor bright! in all things, as well in killing jacks as in trading mules.

But by far the most exciting, as well as exhilarating, mode of pursuit is that with horse and greyhound. Mounted on a fast-flying steed and attended by one or more of these light-legged coursers, the pursuer has about an equal chance with the pursued. There are sporting clubs at Pasadena, Los Angeles and all the principal towns of Southern California. Coursing is a favorite diversion of these organizations, and both ladies and gents participate. California has the finest dogs and horses on the continent, and in the pursuit of these long-eared, light-footed, mischief-making elfs of the soil, many a high mettle is put to the test. The tramp of beating hoofs, the incessant baying of hounds and blowing of horns create a scene of wild excitement and fun without limit. But this is not all. "Good digestion waits on appetite, and health on both." Dyspepsia forgets to practice on you, melancholy abandons his trade and gout looks up another job. The farmer, too, pleased with your operations, invites you to his pomes, and says: "God bless the sport."

CHAPTER IV.

CLIMBING THE SIERRA MADRES.

The writer having been invited to join a select party in the ascent of Mount Wilson, and this invitation promising temporary relief from my friends, who seemed to have no interest in discussing any subject but obstinate jacks, was gracefully accepted. At an early hour, the following morning, all were ready for the much-anticipated trip. The elements composing this mountain-climbing battalion were six in number — a gentleman from England, his wife, two other ladies, the son of a Wisconsin millionaire and the writer. At first I was considerably puzzled to understand why such small potatoes as myself and the Wisconsin chap should have been let into this select circle in such a royal expedition; but before the journey was completed this mystery was cleared up. It appears that this son of the "wild-rushing channel" State had made the trip before, and was therefore a "very convenient accessory to act as guide to the rest of the party. As for myself, there were perhaps other reasons, but as yet I have been able to discover but one, and that will shortly appear.

Scarcely had Aurora mounted her chariot in the East when the chosen six mounted their talaho and dashed away over the plains of the San Gabriel to meet her. But *we* seemed to make the best time, and before the "rosy-fingered daughter of the dawn" had brushed away the ocean mists, our feet were planted on the trail and the great feat of pedestrianism fairly inaugurated. The turn-out, which brought us to the foot of the mountains, returned to the nearest hostelry while its freight of human souls went marching on up the steeps.

In order that the magnitude of this undertaking may be more full appreciated, it should be explained that Mount Wilson is seven thousand feet high and its summit only accessible by means of a narrow footpath between seven and eight miles long. The ascent in many places is very precipitous, and here and there the tourist passes along the edge of precipices from five hundred to perhaps one thousand feet deep. . Very few people have the courage to undertake the journey and still fewer ever succeed in reaching the summit.

With walking sticks in hand we started out at the moderate pace of about one and a quarter miles per hour to make the venturesome jaunt—flagon and snack being strapped to the back of our high-born guide. At this juncture the writer's mission also became apparent. The lordly English gent committed his wife to my care and guidance, and pushed on without ceremony toward the summit. Of course I could not enter protest against this procedure. In fact I had no time. The shuffle was made so adroitly and with so little formality that I did not fairly wake up to the situation until my friend (?) was out of sight and then it was too late. I concluded, therefore, to accept the inevitable as gracefully as I had accepted the optional in

A REFRESHING STREAM

joining the party, and be as gallant and good-natured as though I had not the thought of being made a victim to drudgery. But as we moved on at a moderate gait, slowly surmounting the "rocky steep," I chafed to push forward and make faster progress; but what with the incumbrance of my fair female attendants; what with the increasing heat of the sun and the indisposition of our guide, time rapidly flew, but space seemed practically at a standstill. I became restless and began to feel the weight of the burden on my hands. Not that any fault could be found with the company—for this was select. The Englishman's wife, indeed, was a most charming and estimable young lady, graced with those ornaments of heart and intellect which form the true glory of woman. She had traveled around the world, was communicative, and imparted much valuable information about countries I had never visited. But what of that? These amenities, devoutly to be coveted as they are on ordinary occasions, are nothing to the purpose, when, burning in the bosom, is the all-controlling ambition to reach the top of a mountain. But it was of no use to protest. We pushed on as best we could, gradually increasing our speed, urged at intervals by the censorious voice of our renegade comrade far above us.

After a persevering climb of about two hours and a half we succeeded in reaching the "half-way house," where a snow-fed stream of rejuvenating liquid greeted our famished labials. Here, too, was a hut and a few household utensils — remnants of the personality of a hermit who lived here many years ago.

The dwelling is surrounded by an orchard made up of various kinds of fruit, presenting on the whole an admirable picture for the pen of the romancer. After resting awhile in the mystic shade of this ancient recluse, wondering the while how the stove, which still remained, could have been transported up the mountain which no vehicle could traverse, we resumed the march. There were still about three miles and a half of toilsome climbing before us. But the limpid stream, cool and refreshing, and the means for rest at the old hermitage, had somehow placed the company on a new footing and we advanced a mile or more with renewed energy and courage.

But ho! what's this? Alas! a slide, or sort of quicksand in the trail! Who will venture to cross this? Just to one side is a deep precipice. Should our footing fail we would plunge down forty rods or more among the rocks into irretrievable destruction. Who will venture? We all stood aghast. One of the ladies suggests that as Mr. H. had gone over she thought we would be safe in attempting to cross. Mrs. H. suggests that her husband's getting over safely was no criterion for us, there being no danger of his getting killed until he had reformed. After some deliberation, however, we ventured, and, by clinging to shrubs and roots that projected over the trail, we succeeded in passing this formidable barrier to our progress.

For two hours we pushed onward and upward with good grit, all the time stimulated to persist by the constant delusion that we are within a few rods of the summit. But like the feast prepared for Ixion in Tartarus, this summit continually evaded our covetous grasp just as we were about to revel in its promised delights. It was like ascending a winding staircase or climbing on the thread of an Archimedes screw — lots of distance, little progress. However, at about one o'clock p. m. we reached a summit — but not the highest one. "Isn't this provoking!" exclaims one of the ladies. We are all of one opinion on this point — hence no discussion as to the sentiments severally entertained.

There is another half mile or more to reach the highest peak of Mount Wilson. But the Wisconsin wing of the rear division is completely exhausted and the ladies likewise — no more mountain climbing for them. Refreshments are therefore ordered and, without much deliberation, it is concluded to abandon the balance of the expedition.

But far up in the heights above we hear the incessant calling of our advance guard. The sound comes to us so broken and indistinct that one of the ladies suggests that our deserter may be in trouble. Availing myself of a certain inborn disposition to forgive, I volunteered to go to his rescue. In view of his treasonable conduct in the morning I confess there were no special emotions of love spurring me on to this noble deed. But on general principles and in the interest of humanity I determined to inaugurate a sort of Sir John Franklin expedition to this frozen peak of the Sierra Madres, in search of the lost explorer.

Loading up both internally and externally with

CASCADE IN THE SIERRA MADRES.

suitable refreshments, and taking leave of my fair companions and the foot-sore and broken-winded son of fortune, I pushed off in search of the confidence man, following his foot-tracks in the snow. To fitly describe this part of the trip is not so easy a task. To say that it was laborious would be begging the question. To say that it was a herculean job is not definite. In ascending to the lower summit, we had encountered snow and ice, but there was this difference: The ice down there was cool and wet, dripping like a fresh fried doughnut, while here it was dry and cold. The snow, instead of being six inches deep, was all the way from six feet to six fathoms. The snow, like the ice, was dry and hard. The incline was very steep, and in many places advancement was possible only by kicking the toe of the boot into the hard-crusted snow and climbing as on a ladder. But half the trials of this part of the trip have not been hinted. Many a time I threw myself down exhausted upon a projecting rock or the bare snow itself, puffing like a mouse in a vacuum. Many a time I resolved to abandon further operations and return to my friends below. But this seemed ignominious. At last, however, on reaching a point where the walls of the mountain rose very nearly perpendicularly, I resolved to go no further. At this crisis, reverberating among the pines, rang out more distinctly the voice of the excelsior man, urging me to come on.

"Oh! I'm all right down here," I answered, gasping for breath. "What's the use in going higher? there is scenery enough here if a man doesn't want

THE LAST PULL.

the earth; all I'm after is to find out if you are alive."

"Come on!" again echoed among the pines. "You are almost to the top—a few rods further and you will find it almost level for a quarter of a mile.

"All right," I replied, making a desperate effort to conceal my want of breath. "I'll come right along."

So saying, I began by striking the toes of my boots into the sides of the peak as before, and, grasping the branches of trees and shrubs that projected from the snow, I climbed on, panting all the while like a hounded roe-buck. Time and again I halted on some projecting rock—as often mustered new courage and pressed nobly on." My breathing utensils were now puffing and blowing like a blacksmith's bellows, and my heart thumping like a snare drum. But lo! as I clamber on among the pine trunks I espy the top close by. "Eureka!" One more determined effort and I reach it. "*Venio vinco!* three cheers! I've made it!" A fourth aunt coming to stay all summer couldn't have been more jubilant than I was at that moment, as the gates of heaven literally swung wide open before me.

Running along over the summit some fifty or sixty rods, I discover John Bull standing on a rock at the apex of the mountain, drinking in the scenery with commendable gusto. Extending his hand to help me on to the rock, he exclaims, in wild wonder:

"How, in the name of heaven, did you succeed in getting up here?"

"How, in the name of Rhadamanthos, did you?" I retorted.

"Why! I'm used to such things, but I would have wagered the best horse on Baldwin's ranch that *you* never would have got here."

"*I* never have got here? Great Gaul! if it hadn't

SOUTHERN CALIFORNIA PANORAMA.

been for the women and other baggage, I would have been here hours ago. My only regret now is, that the mountain isn't higher."

Hereupon I intercepted further comment by producing the oranges which distended my pockets and delivering them to my conceited rival. Receiving them with glowing hands, he surrounded them like legerdemain. To watch the poor, faint and famished mountain-scaler as he made these citrous globes "fade like a wreath of mist" before him, was enough to move the heart of a dinothere or make a trilobite sing the national ode. It was really worth the pains of the whole trip. I was, therefore, doubly paid for making the ascent, for it was also well worth the trip to stand there on the pinnacle of the grand old mountain and look out on the universe.

What a panorama! For fifty miles, cities, towns and hamlets; orchards, vineyards, highways and arroyos spread out below us in pigmy proportions. To the rear, nameless spurs and ridges of the Sierra Madres, covered with snow, roll away in the distance till lost in the northern sky. Deep, winding cañons thread the mountains in various directions; valleys bloom with tropical luxuriance below, and the blue Pacific stretches away into the limitless ether, guarded here and there by rocky islands projecting abruptly from the midst of its peaceful waters.

While drinking in the inspiration of these upper realms the descending sun warns us to hasten our downward career. We obey the injunction by bending Spanish bayonets (which grow on the heights) into the form of V and ride down from one declivity to another like shooting stars. There is surely nothing in the category of amusement which compares with the transcendant fun of this style of locomotion. Toboggans and roller-coasters are simply nowhere. It's like getting astride the parabole of a comet and riding triumphantly through space.

Joining the lower detachment of our party just in time to secure the remnants of a lunch basket, we assure our expectant friends that they have lost at least a solid year of real life and advise a hasty retreat. So gathering up our manzanita walking poles, we push downward through chamisal and snow into a milder clime. Soon emerging from the region of snow our senses are again regaled by the cheering sight of larkspurs and lupines, blooming by the way, and the aromatic breath of the valley rising from the mesas and foot-hills beneath us. We descend all the way with gratifying speed and reach the foot of the trail, where our coach is in readiness, just as the sun goes down. The hotel at which we stopped also very nearly went down before we satisfied the cravings superinduced by this excursion to the top of Mount Wilson. Were it not for the opportune arrival of a party of Boston dyspeptics, the institution would surely have collapsed. But it seems to be on a good footing now and the landlord looks encouraged.

VIEW IN SAN ANTONIO CAÑON, ONTARIO, CAL.

CHAPTER V.

RAMBLES BY RAIL.

The next day after a careful diagnosis of our anatomies we concurred in the verdict that traveling by rail was a more approved method of locomotion. Entertaining these sentiments we separated — our English friends embarking for Honolulu, while the secretary, who, the day before, had refused to place his tendons in competition with those of the long-eared burro, joined the writer in making further explorations about the southern part of the state.

These ramblings comprehended a visit to the old Mission at San Gabriel, a town, by the way, that poorly represents the average attractions of a Southern California villa. Here the white cottages of Mexican tenants, glancing in the bright sunlight, their drowsy occupants, strolling listlessly about the verandas, and children lazily swinging upon gates, and hammocks, impressed us with the conviction that we had unmistakably struck a dead municipality. But fearing the coming tourist may imagine that such of the natives as are stretched out in defunct postures are also dead, it might be well to explain that they are only dead drunk. Apart from the Mission, there is little here that is edifying and other Missions on the Coast are quite as interesting. It is, in fact, their historical associations that give them notoriety. After paying our

INSIDE AND OUTSIDE HEADERS.

respects and fees to this antiquated relic of the padres, we availed ourselves of the first opportunity to get out of town.

At Ontario, a few miles to the east, on the Southern Pacific, such a strange contrast is presented that we were as much concerned about leaving as we had lately been in being laid off among the forbidding exhibitions of squalid San Gabriel. In the vicinity of this place, Ontario, there are a number of cañons of remarkable beauty leading into the Sierra Madres. These the tourist should visit. Here, too is probably the finest eucalyptus avenue in Southern California. In its refreshing shade one enjoys a country drive along a thoroughfare possessing elements of beauty of which its rival Euclid can not boast. The mountain scenery between Ontario and Riverside is probably also unrivaled in Southern California. Cucumonga, San Jacinto and Old Baldy (the latter two miles high) all lift their snowy coronets with royal dignity and the lesser peaks seem to vie with each other in vain efforts to scale the firmament.

Pomona, the noted orange town, and San Bernardino, whose flowing artesian wells are visible from the railroad, are both on the line and the latter is much visited by people from abroad.

At Riverside the tourist wanders literally through miles of orange groves, and (if no dogs or vigilance committees intervene) he safely plucks from fragrant boughs large and luscious pendants of saporific gold.

From this fruit and floral paradise we proceeded back to the coast, where we more sensibly detected the

subtle sea breeze, distilling its vaporous tonic, and where we watched with emotion the huge porpoise rolling in the surf. But men and boys seemed also to enjoy the briny deep equally well with the porpoise. A hot sea bath is another seaside luxury, especially to the invalid and those of delicate constitutions. The tonic effect of these ablutions is such that one really forgets his old-time prejudice against water. Even the man who took the worst cold of his life in his last bathing operation twenty-eight years ago, seems enthusiastic over these briny recreations.

The chief coast resorts of Southern California are, in order from the south, San Diego, Santa Monica, Santa Barbara and Monterey — all saints but one, and this has the distinction of a name that makes it King's Mountain. All of them are full of interest. all have the usual seaside attractions — fine hotels, ample facilities for bathing, boating, yachting, and all the ordinary means of amusement and diversion.

Monterey, the early capital of California, commonly classed as a Southern California town, is most conveniently reached from San Francisco — the Southern Pacific having put on the fastest train of the State, reaching this noted resort, a distance of one hundred and twenty-five miles, in three and a half hours. The Del Monte Hotel near by has a world-wide reputation. It is in the midst of beautiful parks, verdant lawns and floral gardens, everything being tropical and suggestive of affluence and beauty. It is easily reached from Monterey by an excellent macadamized road that passes through Pacific and Cypress Groves, by the old Mission and these places.

VIEW FROM CASTLE ROCK, NEAR SANTA BARBARA.

Santa Cruz, the most frequented by San Franciscans of any of the Pacific Coast towns, is also on Monterey Bay, but at the opposite end. Added to the usual seaside attractions are the noted redwoods near by, called the "big trees," one of which is three hundred feet high and sixty feet around,— thus approaching in magnitude the big trees proper.

In the vicinity of these resorts in the mountains of the Coast Range nature has indeed been lavish with her arboreal attractions. Just as the farmer finds a depth and variety of soil unknown in the East, so here the botanist finds in his favorite field of study a wealth and diversity of vegetable growths unapproached by any other State in the Union.

The mossy, gnarled, tough-fibered Monterey cypress, growing upon rocks close by the sea, is one of the many interesting vegetable curiosities of this locality. It is in fact the only specimen of the kind known except one other at another point on the coast.

In this region, also flourishes the eucalyptus, or Australian blue-gum, so universal in the settled portions of Southern California. This is a truly representative tree of the Pacific Slope. It grows so rapidly that within the limits of half a dozen years, it becomes a respectable shade-producer, acquiring a magnitude that strikingly suggests the rapid growth of a boom town.

The madrona, or arbutus, is another remarkable specimen. Its bark is as smooth and clean cut as the persuasion of a land agent, and the tree has a grace of attitude and motion from the study of which an actress might profit. Yet with all its grace and beauty, it is

SCENE IN THE COAST RANGE.

not a pigmy in its kingdom, one specimen near San
Francisco being twenty-three feet in circumference.
The species often grows to the height of one hundred
feet, throwing out in every direction its lithe and
mystic branches laden with cream-tinted blossoms.

But, while this whole region is replete with peculiar
and noted representatives of the vegetable kingdom,
fair and fascinating, it is the omnipresence of the
various varieties of oak that most surprise the tourist
from abroad. It would be in vain to attempt to cata-
logue these, or give the reader an adequate idea of
their propensity to assume shapes, postures and colo-
cations that seem specially designed to please. I have
seen lawns and parks and promenades laid out by
nature and ornamented with these trees that would put
to route the labored efforts of the cleverest arboricul-
turist.

Here too are to be seen pines almost as various and
diverse as the ubiquitous oak, some of which are found
growing at the water's edge. The pines of the Sierras
however, outdo those of the Coast Range, and to these
majestic dwellers of the heights, I shall have occasion
to allude in connection with the Sequoias of the giant
forests.

The odoriferous laurel and aromatic nutmeg, in
certain groves of this vicinity, are also to be found,
making the tourist imagine that he is in the heart of
the tropics instead of thirteen degrees over the line
into the temperate zone.

Southern California, whether on the coast or in the
cheerful valleys of the southern counties, must be con-

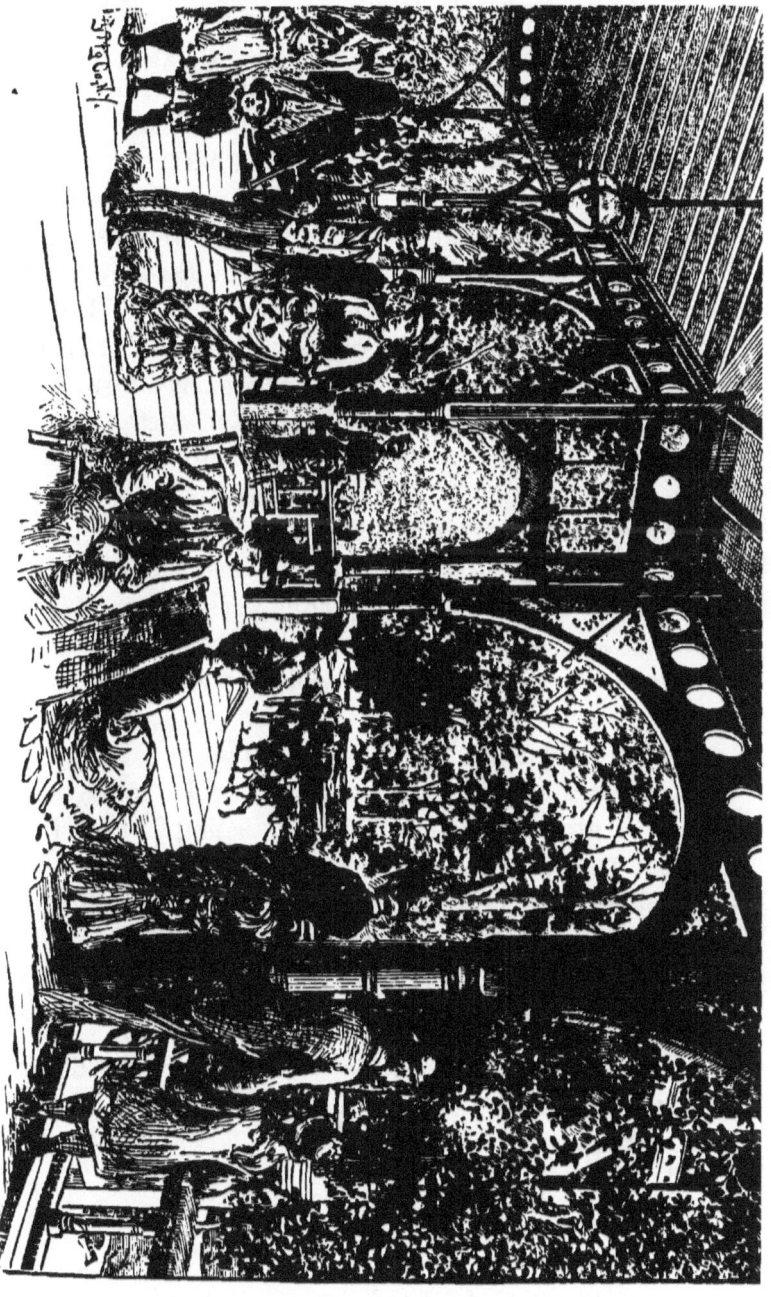

TROPICAL LUXURIANCE—DEL MONTE.

ceded many paradisaical characteristics, at least in winter. Allowing that there are months when everything appears parched and dry, that dusty roads and sandstorms *do* exist, that water is dear and prices of real estate scheduled in a way to puzzle and perplex, still there are the balm and sunshine, the fruits and flowers and halcyon days that can not, by the subtilties of logic be disrobed of their healthful charms. Everywhere we find daily reminders of the luxuriant growth, the romantic scenery and the rapturous skies once so faithfully depicted by the lamented author of "Ramona." Here are the hills and mesas and mountains, the sands and arroyos, the cañons and snow-fed crystal streams; here flourish not only the vine and fig tree, but also the lanceolate olive, the flowering almond, the orange and lemon, blending their green and gilt in pleasing tints, and even the "golden pomegranates of Eden" decked in the rich caparison of scarlet blossoms and blushing fruit. Here, too, in delightful villas and cheerful homes one catches unbidden the perfume of geranium and rose, while stealing in upon the unguarded senses like an unseen spirit comes the ravishing breath of jasmine and stephanotis—all this when, in the chilly East, locked in ice and snow,

> "Coughing drowns the parson's saw,
> And Marion's nose looks red and raw."

The coughing is also to be found here, but this is largely imported. Long live the winters of Southern California.

CHAPTER VI.

INTO THE HEART OF THE SIERRAS.

There is only one Yosemite Valley, and only one trip to this enchanted reserve ever made exactly after the fashion of the one in which the writer was implicated.

My associates in this excursion among the Sierras were an Ohio real estate operator (who has lately removed to California), the private secretary of an eminent New York official, and a Chicago merchant. These, whom I have already alluded to, have constituted the *dramatis personæ* in a number of successful exploits here on the Pacific coast. Knowing, from common report, that the wonders of the Yosemite are more or less overpowering in their nature, and reasoning that four would offer more resistance than one, it was only fair to suppose that the shock to our sensibilities would be proportionately lessened by being thus distributed over this increased amount of surface. If *one* couldn't stand it, *four* surely could. So we decided to form another league, forgetful of past aggrievances. Organizing as the " California Mutual Protective Alliance for Resisting the Overpowering Effects of Wild Flourishes of Natural Scenery," we set out prepared for any emergency. Conscious of the newly--created powers with which we had become vested by our corporate name, we bade adieu to the " City of the

Queen of Angels," to which we had but recently returned from the coast, and the Southland to which we had become more or less endeared, and with good courage pushed northward by the Southern Pacific Railway through the cheerful San Fernando valley. Crossing the desolate Mojave desert near the dry lakes, where in the vegetable world, juniper and bunch-grass, dwarf cedar, greecewood and the Yucca palm hold undisputed sway, we entered the Tehachepi mountains in high colors. Swinging around the famous "Loop," among chaparral-crowned hills and gypsum ridges, and witnessing the most wonderful feats of engineering in the State, we soon reached the great valley of the San Joaquin.

Making short stop-offs at Bakersfield, the capital of Kern county, and Fresno, the center of the raisin-making industry, we gathered some useful information respecting the business interests and mode of life in these places. In our drives into the country we found something worthy of comment in the vast fields of alfalfa and grain, the thousands of sheep grazing on hillsides and "hog-wallows," and the sleek herds of horses and cattle roving on the plains.

The ubiquitous jack-rabbit, too, is here — more abounding, in fact, than in the south — to the grief of the ranchman and hardly to the joy of the sportsman, since they are really too plenty to make the chase exciting. The inhabitants have resorted to various devices to exterminate this persistent race of mischief-makers, a common method being to steal upon them in an ox-cart bearing heavy musketry. While this mode is not

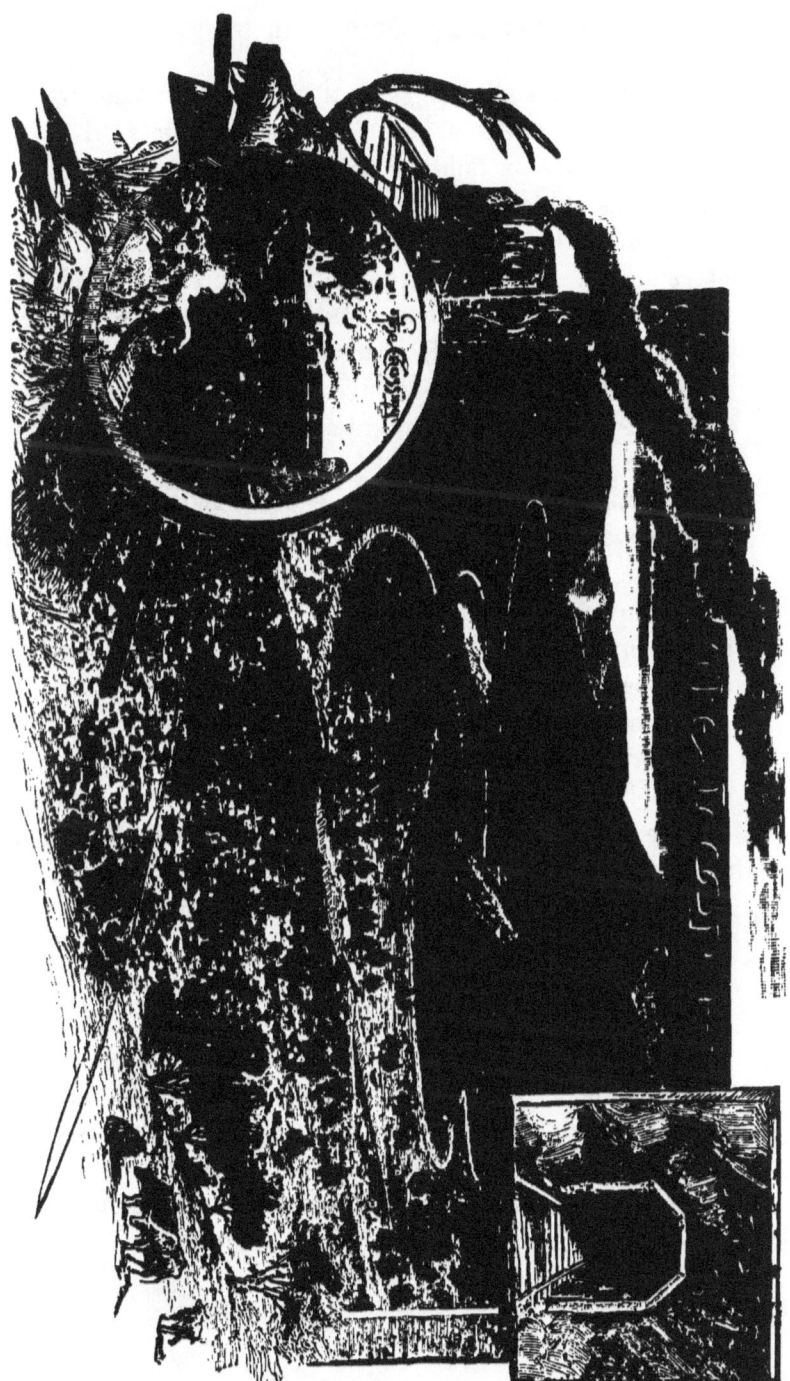

THE LOOP.

according to the golden rule, it is very effectual in weakening the ranks of these deluded lightfoots, who, shy of men, are on familiar terms with roving herds and moving vehicles. Formerly this method was much in vogue, the booty thus secured being shipped to the city markets. Rabbit drives are now more approved. By this plan neighborhoods turn out *en masse* and pursue the pests from all quarters of the horizon into a large corral built to receive them — the pursuers hemming them in and slaughtering them by the hundreds, or perhaps thousands.

Leaving Fresno and vicinity we resumed our northward movements toward the point of departure for the Yosemite. This was an interesting ride through the San Joaquin, presenting, as it did, phases differing in important respects from anything yet seen. Everything seems to be numbered by the thousand here. The ranches contain thousands of acres; sheep and cattle are herded by the thousand; thousands of geese and rabbits and cranes prey upon the crops. But what engaged our interest most were the thousand snow-clad peaks of the Sierras, looming up before us with lordly airs and warning us of the mysteries on exhibition over beyond.

At a small station some one hundred miles from the famous valley we disembarked and secured a livery, having decided upon this means of transit to secure greater freedom in our movements. Besides, the Ohio capitalist's southern real estate having taken a set-back during the past year or two, the rest of the party felt it to be an imperative duty to reprove his customary extravagance and teach him a lesson in economy. To this end we diligently inquired of the German hostler of whom we procured our conveyance, how much this trip would set us back financially. The attending stable boy having interpreted our interrogatories to "Cousin Michael" the latter responded in true German style:

"Vell, I toldt you all aboudt how it vas. Wie lang bist du in dose Yosemitees?"

"O, we want to be gone about ten days."

"Vell. I vill tell you boudt dot. I make it sheap, genook. Ven you get pack I tole you all aboudt dot price."

After insisting upon knowing the price before we started, "Mynheer Closh" finally yields to our demands and says:

"I will make dose oxpenses sheap mit you—I scharge you noor foonf-sick tollars."

Having about two hundred miles to drive among the hills and mountains we could not go amiss on this price and so without chaffering agreed to pay "Mynheer" the fifty dollars for his best rig. The latter, pleased that the bargain was consummated, at this point threw in a little free advice with the evident purpose of giving us the full worth of our money.

"I tole you sumdings vot safe you oxpenses undt I vill tole you dot mitoudt scharging nottings," continued clever "Closh." "Dose rates mit dem Yosemite hotels vas four tollar ein day, aber you make him sheaper some ven you dond't put too much shtyle on already yet."

"How's that?"

"Vell, I tole you how it comes aboudt. Dose hotel fellers puts the price vay *oop* to fellers mit shtyle on, undt vay *down* to fellers mitout der shtyle."

I, for one, being in for economy skirmished around and secured a slouch hat, which, after considerable

THE FLUME.

heated discussion on the part of my comrades, was decided to be a trifle worse than the one I discarded. I tried persistently, but in vain, to induce the rest of the company to follow my example, arguing earnestly and logically that this change in the habiliments of my upper story would save the company at least eight dollars a day on board, and probably not less than one

A SIERRA CASCADE.

dollar and fifty cents a bushel on oats; and that if they would do as I had done this reduction would be perceptibly larger. I especially insisted that the Ohio real estate operator should, in view of his depreciated city lots, be consistent and lower the standard of his wearing apparel. But all logic was in vain. Each one declared that I had already lowered the standard of dress at least ninety per cent. for the whole party, and that if any reduction of rates were to be had on this basis my slouch hat would secure them. But time was passing, and I succumbed to the decision of the majority, waving my plea for dress reform, conscious of having made enough objections to the course of my opponents to place them on the defensive should anything betide us. After taking these advisable precautions I thus allowed the "deadlock," which was clogging the wheels of progress, to be broken, having become thoroughly ingratiated into the affections of my bucolic constituency.

We then started off under a favorable sky toward the mountains, all divergences of opinion being either reconciled or tolerated. We were, at least, all harmonious on one point, and that was: to reach the valley. Rain, shine or earthquake, we were bound for the far-famed Yosemite. How we did fly! Over hills, down into the valleys, up the mountains, away into the heart of the Sierras.

Space will not admit of a detailed account of the first two days' drive, In general, however, it may be said that much that was instructive delighted both eye and ear, and equally as much that was entertaining proved highly edifying. Here were sheep and cattle feeding upon a thousand hills. Here were variously colored rocks strewed along the vales and crowning the hill-tops. Here were abandoned shafts and for-

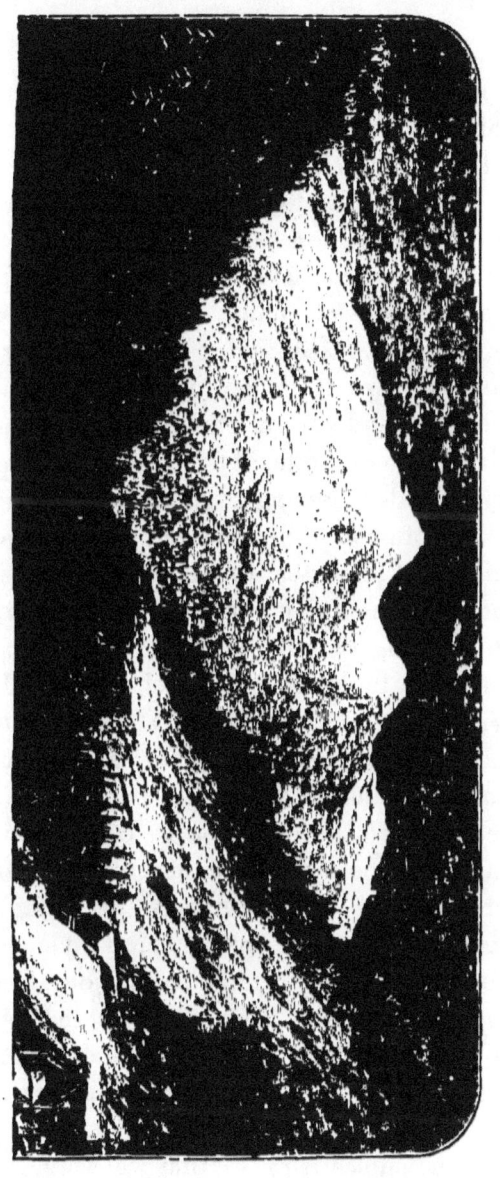

SUMMITS OF THE SIERRA NEVADAS.

saken mining camps. Here, too, was the long flume for rafting lumber, winding like a gargantuan boa around the mountain peaks for many miles. At Grub Gulch (a name dear to the heart of the average prospector, since tradition has it that he could make his "grub" here when he failed everywhere else) there were a number of mines in successful operation. These we duly visited, taking away with us several desirable specimens of gold ore. We also encountered deer en route and several other denizens of the forest to which we found difficulty in affixing the appropriate names. While referring to game it is also worthy to note the profusion of pigeons and quails inhabiting the foot-hills. At least ten thousand of these, started by the sound of our flying wheels, encountered our path within shooting range — enough, properly served up, to have stood the priests of Israel over Sunday in the wilderness, or, if served up according to modern formula, to have made soup for Xenophon and his army of ten thousand during the period of their retreat — one barrel of the emulsion to each soldier. Bagging a few of these tender-loined bipeds, I endeavored to persuade my swell partners to "rough it" and cook our own game in genuine camp style. But there was no use in trying to force lessons of economy upon my flush attendants. They were opposed to anything which might soil their knee-buckles and so the quails were ordered served up on toast at the tavern.

But without detailing these and similar episodes of the journey, suffice it to say that we were, during this part of the trip, elated, benighted, snowed on, hailed and thundered at by turns. On one occasion Jupiter Pluvius, after smashing up our umbrellas in a violent gale, turned the hose on the whole crowd. But still we sped on like pursued road-runners until after two days of eventful sight-seeing, fusillading and crack driving among the pine-studded heights of the Sierras, we arrived at Big Tree Station, about two-thirds of the distance to the valley. Here we put up for the night, having stopped the first night at Grub Gulch.

Big Tree Station is on the Yosemite Reserve. So now we had to deal with the government and pay government prices. I knew the schedule rates to be four dollars a day, but in view of "Mynheer's" friendly admonitions in regard to style it was only fair to conclude that I was entitled to "cut rates." So, after a good night's rest and an ample breakfast, all feeling in good spirits for another day's drive, I ordered our rig and stepped up to the office to pay the bill. Pulling the slouch hat well down on to my head and twisting my necktie askew over the collar I struck an attitude and enquired, in true western phraseology, as to the amount of tax the government proposed to levy on me and my "pards."

"Supper, lodging and breakfast for four — and horse feed, fifteen dollars sir," was the consoling reply.

Being assured that this included tooth-picks and all, I paid the bill like a lord, knowing this to be the regular rate to tourists, and that it was futile to persist in trying to convey the impression of poverty with the Ohio capitalist and his plug hat looming up in our midst. It was equally preposterous to think of posing

ENTRANCE TO YOSEMITE VALLEY.

as local patronage with our names registered from three different states. We were here at about the same altitude as the Yosemite, but must overcome one thousand six hundred feet to reach it. We were good for this, and so boarding our barouche courageously dashed away into the interminable depths of forest before us. I now used all the power of persuasion I could muster to induce my co-travelers to smash in the tops of their stiff hats, arguing that it would save many times the value of their head-gear in the cost of living. But all rhetoric was in vain. The nabobs recklessly persisted in preserving the original shapes of their skull-protectors thus compelling me to unjustly share the loss which must ensue as a logical sequence of their pig-headedness. But never mind, Rome wasn't reformed in a day.

Crack! goes the rattan, and onward we speed through forests of pine, cedar and redwood. Away we fly over dizzy heights, along precipitous banks, down one hill and up two, until we reach the summit. Here we took dinner at a trapper's, there being no hotel between Big Trees and the Yosemite.

During our repast we learned something of the peculiar life of this solitude. Among other interesting incidents of the place, there was once a herd of deer roving about in these mountain wilds, that made it a part of the daily programme to visit the old cabin on the summit. Having here received their usual allowance of salt and regaled their appetites at the festive slop-pail, they returned to their mountain fastnesses, seemingly satisfied with the bill of fare provided by their good-natured host. These, too, were the feelings which we entertained, as we took our leave and sped away down the heights along a precipitous trail toward the valley. After advancing several miles we reached an opening in the almost interminable forest, whence our eyes were greeted by another beautiful panorama of mountain scenery. Beyond the deep, picturesque gorge, on the verge of which the mountain roadway extends for several miles, could be seen hills and mountains rolling away, one above another, far in the distance, and even the Coast Range, at least a hundred miles to the west, standing in dim outline against the sky. But behold! What is this? All at once we reach the height overlooking the valley. A sign-board discloses the fact that we are on the Peak of Inspiration. It is, however, a precipice rather than a peak. But in the matter of inspiration there could be no question, as the Yosemite unfolded its robes of matchless beauty before us.

CHAPTER VII.

EARTH'S CROWNING GLORY.

Here, facing us from the opposite side of the valley, is a huge promontory of granite, having smooth, polished sides, handsomely striped with peculiar tints of light and shade, and rising to the height of fifteen Bunker Hill monuments or seven of Egypt's highest pyramids. This we at once recognized as the El Capitan of which Prof. Whitney wrote: "It is doubtful if anywhere in the world is presented so squarely cut, so lofty and so imposing a face of rock." As we stand looking in wonder at this massive pile, a beautiful silvery cloud settles down upon its summit and presents, in the light of the sinking sun, a halo of indescribable beauty crowning the "great chief of the valley." Descending along a tortuous trail in the form of a winding stair-case, we soon cross the path of the "rock avalanche" that recently tore up trees, breaking them into fragments and creating the wildest imaginable scene of destruction. As we reach Pohono bridge, at the foot of the trail, the beautiful Bridal Veil appears in full glory, sifting its waters over a precipice nearly one thousand feet above the valley. In falling, it breaks into a shower of mist that is so deflected by currents of air as to present the appearance of a white silken veil tossed in the wind. On the opposite side of the valley the Ribbon or Virgin Tears Fall plunges, in a slender stream, over the head of El Capitan and breaks into a mist that, to all appearances, loses itself in the air before it has completed a third of its journey. The upper part of this miniature fall being obscured by the nebulous halo resting on El Capitan, the novel spectacle is presented of a delicate cascade falling directly from the clouds.

Three massive monoliths, called the Three Brothers, now rise up before us — the highest six hundred feet above El Capitan. Now Cathedral Rock and its two graceful spires loom into view, reaching heights before which Trinity and St. Patrick's would appear like pigmies in the presence of Hercules. Anon "The Sentinel" appears — a colossal granite obelisk perched upon an eminence two thousand feet above the valley, and rising above this fifteen times the height of Cleopatra's needle. Wonder follows upon wonder, and all at once the Yosemite Falls breaks into full view, facing the giant Sentinel and pouring its restless, roaring waters over a precipice half a mile above our heads or more than sixteen times the height of Niagara. The highest portion of its white, feathery column is soon enveloped in a cumbrous cloud of mist, and again we have the marvelous sight of a cataract falling directly from the heavens.

Reaching the old Yosemite Valley House, shortly before dark we enjoyed from its historic veranda a fine view of the Yosemite falls, pouring over a precipice two thousand five hundred and forty-eight feet above the valley, the precipice being about a thousand feet below the tops of the ledges enclosing it. The valley

YOSEMITE IN EARLY TIMES.

itself is about four thousand feet above the sea and enclosed by nearly perpendicular walls as much higher.

The Duke of Sutherland, who visited the valley a few years ago, said: "The Yosemite spoils one for any other scenery upon earth." According to this, the writer and his comrades spent several days deliberately and perseveringly spoiling themselves for the average attractions of this earth.

In our perambulations the day following our arrival we passed the old Hutchins cabin with which so many historical events pertaining to the opening of the valley are associated. Here are still to be seen the ancient cooking stove, the dilapidated chairs and broken crockery that did such commendable service "in the days that are gone." Beyond this, a short distance, we reached the base of the lower Yosemite fall, in approaching which were encountered the wind currents produced by the falling waters. These swept upward under umbrellas and outer garments in the form of a baptismal spray that was most effective. A brief encampment before the cheerful fire-place at the hotel, however, removed any inconveniences we might suffer from this source, and after dinner we were prepared to continue our explorations.

These consisted chiefly of a twenty-mile drive about the valley, including the trip to the cascades, some eight miles down the river. In this direction we were confronted by numberless massive rocks, weighing hundreds of tons, and scattered promiscuously along the banks of the river for several miles. These were perched up in all manner of perilous attitudes, many of them being piled one above another in tumble down positions—here overhanging the roadways and there set up on end some distance above us, freighted with disaster. We knew full well that others by thousands had made the tour of the valley unharmed and all reason seemed to indicate that the chances of getting through alive were in our favor. It was, nevertheless, impossible to dispel the

BRIDAL VEIL FALL

CATHEDRAL ROCKS.

conviction that these mountain-sized rocks, so insecurely poised above us, would come tearing down the declivities and put an end to our recreations. Occasionally one of these does actually lose its anchorage and the devastating result is frightful. While nothing could be more fear-inspiring than this journey down the river, few sights could be better calculated to excite wonder than the return trip. In the latter the attention is somewhat withdrawn from these threatening boulders and directed to the imposing wall of masonry, half a mile high, that hems in the valley on both sides, and

THE SENTINEL.

over the rim or summit of which numerous cascades fall in picturesque beauty.

Here the wildest and most fairy-like scenes break upon the vision. The day we made the trip in this direction nature seemed to have on her high-heeled shoes, and was in all respects dressed as if for some special occasion. The massive granite walls of the valley seemed larger and larger the more minutely they were scanned, and after we had advanced a short distance the very heavens fell in the form of descending clouds, here resting upon the rocky walls of the valley and in places falling far below into the valley itself. Trees and mountain peaks, three thousand feet above us, appeared through rifts in the clouds, as if standing isolated and alone in the clear sky. Scores of delicate cascades were, for all our senses could discover, falling directly from heaven and everywhere the goddess of enchantment held undisputed sway.

The next day we ordered our rig at an early hour and proceeded to explore the valley in the opposite direction, or up the river. Some two miles above the hotels we found the Merced divided into three branches, which retreat in the form of rocky cañons into the mysterious wilds of the Sierras. To trace these cañons up toward their sources was our purpose.

Beginning at the left branch, called the Tenaya Fork, we drove over a meandering road two miles up the cañon. Of the highway itself little can be said except that it failed to keep the same point of compass or level for any considerable distance. But for all this it faithfully performed its office in bringing us to the small but charming sheet of water that lay so snugly ensconced among the mountains at its terminus. This is the much-talked-of Mirror Lake, in whose silver waters are reflected mountain peaks that rise abruptly

YOSEMITE FALLS.

from its margin nearly a mile high. We were especially fortunate in the time selected for viewing this phenomenon. The sun, just rising over South Dome, Mount Watkins and other tree-studded peaks, as seen reflected in the smooth surface of the lake, all combined to produce a sublime effect. Just over the lake a curious conformation of outlines and peculiar blending of colors unite to form two novel pictures on the adjacent rocks — the one resembling white garments suspended on a clothes-line, and the other a woman's head. The latter is called the "Goddess of the Valley."

Returning to the forks of the river and omitting the ascent of the Illilouette or southwest fork, whose chief object of interest — the Illilouette Falls — is visible from a point on the main branch, we dismount and proceed on foot up the Nevada trail. This winds along the banks of the main river and affords many charming views *en route* to the more noted points of interest five miles up the trail. A persevering climb of three miles brings us to Register Rock, near which a good view is obtained of Vernal Falls. Continuing the ascent over rocks and crags and amid a galaxy of wondrous sights and sounds, we soon pass through the mists of the falls, climb "The Ladder," and at last reach the precipice over which the waters of the Merced fall three hundred and fifty feet. Fortune favors the fearless, and here, projecting out from among the rocks above, we espy the hospitable roof of Snow's Hotel, the supplies of which are brought on horseback over a precipitous bridle path five miles in length.

MIRROR LAKE.

After renewing our drooping energies at this mountain refectory, we proceeded to the precipice overlooking Vernal Falls. Here we find ourselves in one of Nature's grandest temples — hemmed in on all sides by an amphitheatre which has probably no parallel on the continent, if anywhere in the world. A monstrous flat rock, perhaps an eighth of a mile long and half as wide, forms a spacious rostrum over which the ob-

NORTH DOME.

server may wander at pleasure. Another, similar to this, only turned up on end, rises hundreds of feet out of the depths, protruding just far enough above the horizontal one to form a secure breastwork along the edge of the precipice. One is thus enabled to approach to the very brink of the falls without peril. The praises of Yosemite are variously sung as seen from Inspiration and Glacier Point, at the foot of Bridal Veil and the summit of Sentinel Dome and Eagle Peak; but if comparisons are in order amid a host of wonderful sights, all of which seem a consummation of crowning glories, this part of the valley surely deserves the palm as presenting the beau ideal of true loveliness in nature combined with awful sublimity. The ample collation provided our company by the considerate old gentleman who presides over this sequestered inn, so remote from human habitation, certainly could not account for the favorable impression produced by the environments of the place.

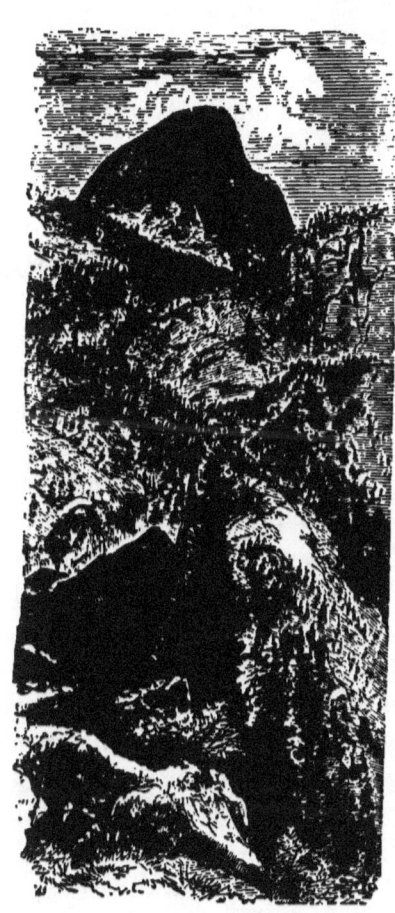
SOUTH DOME.

At the right the Merced River glides noiselessly along its unruffled bed and suddenly hurls its full volume of water over the precipice at your feet and far down into the abyss before your eyes. But before it is fairly lodged in these mysterious depths, it throws out a cloud of mist that is borne hundreds of feet into the air by ascending currents, presenting a continual succession of rainbows to the observer standing in the sunlight below. No sooner are these waters marshalled into their channel than they plunge violently down their ragged bed, dashing among rocks and roots, and broken trunks of hemlock and fir, here breaking into feathery shafts and there shooting perpendicularly into the air, boiling, seething and glancing in the sunlight. On either side of this restless flood nearly perpendicular walls of granite rise to the height of three or four thousand feet, and present a beautiful combination of colors. Directly in front, rising over three thousand feet above the valley, is a beautiful triangular glacis crowned with evergreens. In this direction Grizzly Peak and Glacier Point loom up in grand proportions. The waters dash and roar on every side, and a train of other sights and sounds falls upon eye and ear, bewildering sense and leading the mind away from self to a consciousness of higher powers that seem to preside over the place.

Turning to the rear and looking up the river, a view no less enchanting greets the eye. Here the Nevada Falls, also containing the entire volume of the main river, show their white flashing waters as they shoot downward seven hundred feet to the river bed below. Here, gathering themselves within their wonted channel, they dash furiously down among the rocks, forming the beautiful Diamond Cascades.

VIEWS IN THE VALLEY.

Thence spreading out over the surface of a spacious, flat rock, they flow on as composedly as if nothing had happened, serenely collecting themselves at your side, into a miniature crystal lake. Here, resting a moment, as it were, they make the second mad plunge over the Vernal precipice just described.

From this outlook the more distant view is no less inspiring. South Dome shows his snowy summit a mile above the valley. Mount Broderick lifts heavenward his imperious head, and Starr King triumphantly displays his pine-crowned temples nine thousand feet above the sea. Near by is the Cap of Liberty, standing forth like a guardian of the centuries, raising his mighty granite shaft above us more than ten times the height of the dome of the capitol at Washington.

But here I might as well surrender at discretion. To attempt to convey an adequate conception of these wonderful manifestations, or as some call them "marvelous freaks," would be presumption. To describe them in detail would be to describe the kaleidoscopic scenes of an ever-shifting panorama. The constant wonder is that the same object of interest impresses the observer so differently at different times. This was especially noticeable on our return from the upper portion of the valley. The three domes, Grizzly and Glacier peaks, Illilouette Falls and the splashing, glistening waters of the Merced all assumed a new garb of glory in the light of the setting sun. Washington Column and North Dome posed in spectral colors, new and strange, and the Royal Arches assumed

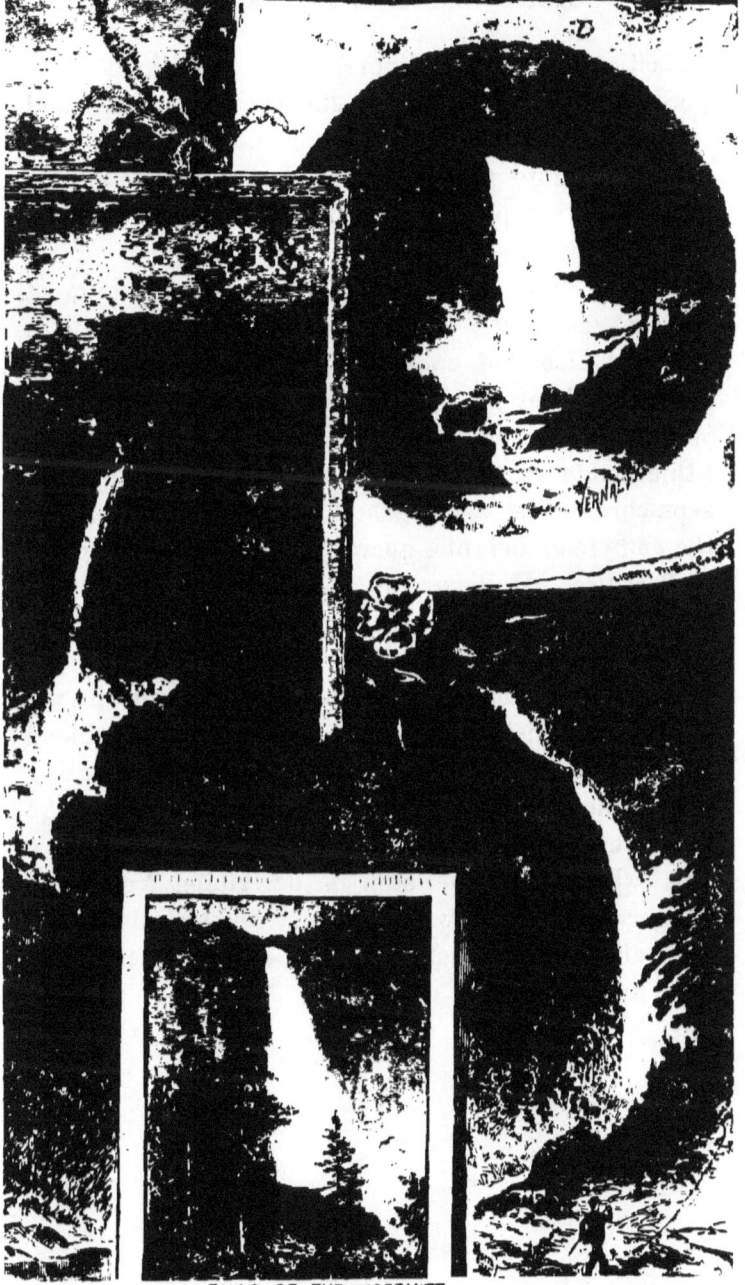
FALLS OF THE YOSEMITE

fantastic phases which favored the superstition that we were about to enter the mystic confines of a Druid temple. The summit of the half dome was isolated from its granite pedestal by an ascending cloud, and thus made to appear like the inverted hulk a foundered ship drifting at sea.

The observer at Yosemite is the happy victim of constant surprise. He stands before El Capitan in mute astonishment, contemplating the stupendous proportions of a single granite rock two miles long and two-thirds of a mile high. He sees the great monolithic giants of the earth here resurrected from the sepulchre of the ages, standing mute sentinels before the empyrean heights, guarding, as it were, the gates of Paradise. He hears the deep intonations of surging floods at his feet and the weird music of clashing waters half a mile above his head. He catches the mystic notes, sung by miniature cascades high in the clouds and listens in rapt wonder, as they blend their choral voices with the winds of heaven, chanting wild anthems to the granite hosts, that stand from age to age, unwearied listeners to their ceaseless rhapsodies. But where shall we stop in describing Yosemite? Niagara herself throws up the white flag in attempting to rival it and so must every writer who attempts to describe it.

AMONG THE PINES OF THE SIERRAS.

CHAPTER VIII.

THE MAMMOTH TREES.

In the last chapter I alluded to the "Mammoth Trees of California," within a few miles of which we passed on our way to the Yosemite. In making the trip to the Yosemite by stage, it is generally thought advisable to go by one route and return by another, but the necessity of getting our rig and accessories back to the point of departure on the Southern Pacific, and gathering up the few worldly effects which we had left at that place, compelled us to go and return by the same route. By so doing, however, we were enabled to study the wonderful flora of the Sierras more in detail, and especially to visit the Mariposa grove of "Big Trees." Notwithstanding the familiar aspect of the way, there was still more or less of the constant wonder, "What next?" and we were all the while on the lookout for some new extravaganza in nature. In this we were eminently favored in our explorations among the "Big Trees." Arriving at "Big Tree" station the same day that we left the valley, we there put up for the night. In good season the following morning we pushed off for the Sequoia forest. As these prodigies of the vegetable kingdom are to be found only at altitudes ranging from five to seven thousand feet, we were obliged to make a considerable ascent to reach them. In so doing we encountered snow from two to three feet deep, but the road somewhat broken by the stage enabled us without great difficulty to make the journey. Although the main body of the grove is eight miles from the hotel, we

MEASURING THE GRIZZLY GIANT.

had scarcely advanced half that distance when we found ourselves in the midst of trees of unusual size — perhaps twelve to fifteen feet in diameter. This phenomena was viewed as an appropriate introduction to the greater marvels beyond, which we were fondly anticipating, and concerning which so many Quixotic stories have been told.

The trees passed in the outskirts of the grove resembled large, shapely cedars, though taller and more imposing. They did not appeal to the senses as being exactly marvelous; still they surpassed any variety of the pine family we had yet seen, and furnished a very suggestive hint of what was coming. As we advanced, the trunks continued to assume more and more conspicuous proportions, until we reached the "Grizzly Giant," the largest tree in the grove. This is advertised as being thirty-three feet in diameter; but, according to my own measurements, these figures must be considered as applying to its longest diameter, which includes a gnarled protuberance of about two feet in thickness. Its height is two hundred and sixty feet, its circumference ninety-four, and at a distance of one hundred feet from the ground is a limb six feet through. According to conservative estimate, the "Grizzly Giant" must have been a thrifty young tree when the Children of Israel were wandering in the Desert of Sinai. At the beginning of the Christian Era it must have towered aloft nearly to its present height. These trees, being so far above their neighbors, are exposed to the surging elements of the upper regions, and are thus constantly trimmed and broken down at their summits by wind and accumulating snow, so that many of the finest specimens are truncated and present a dwarfish appearance. The "Grizzly Giant" has suffered in this respect even

THE WAWONA.

more than its weaker brethren, besides having been assailed by forest fires. But in spite of all its misfortunes and adversities, it still remains a titanic wonder of the vegetable world—the Antæus of the palestra—for forty centuries a wrestler with lightning and tempest, and to-day proud, defiant, and boldly awaiting its rival, Hercules. I, for one, was glad to scrape acquaintance with the veteran wrestler with the winds, and treated him with perfect confidence; but my friend, the Secretary, eyed the old giant with suspicion and expressed doubts about his age. He said the old fellow didn't look as old as he was cracked up to be, and, in order to satisfy his skepticism on this point, gathered a number of his cones, with the express purpose of planting them on his return to the East. As soon as the Secretary's investigations are completed, the true age of a tree thirty feet in diameter will be duly reported.

After a careful and respectful survey of the old giant's anatomy we proceeded to pay our respects to the lesser dignitaries of the Big Tree Forest. These, though less prodigious, were able to make themselves interesting — in some cases manifesting a remarkable spirit of hospitality, even inviting us inside. Most of them bear familiar names. There is "Longfellow," "Whittier," "Harvard," "The Faithful Couple," "Virginia," and "Maryland" (close by each other's side); "The Diamond Group" of four, "The Sentinels," "The Eight Commissioners," "Lincoln," "Grant," "Illinois," "Columbia," and other noted ones whose names I do not chance to recall. The once imperious "Andy Johnson" fell about a dozen years ago. But the tree above all others which seems to attract attention is the "Wawona," through which the stage drives in making the circuit of the grove. Under this we halted long enough to observe that the roof above us was amply sufficient to cover our horses and

HOLLOW TRUNK.

vehicle, with awning to spare, the distance through being twenty-eight feet. Near this was the "Pioneer's Cabin," a hollow, upright tree, capable of housing a dozen or more persons peaceably inclined. Not far from this was a prostrate hollow trunk, which the writer entered, walking upright, some distance before being able to reach the roof above.

In the grove there are fully six hundred trees from thirty to ninety feet in circumference and from two hundred and twenty-five to three hundred feet in height. It is the only grove set aside as a national park — all the others, seven in number, being private property. Some of the latter, however, are quite as remarkable, though but one of them — the Calaveras — is visited to any considerable extent by tourists. This is owing to their being less accessible and not kept in shape to receive company. The largest tree yet discovered is in Tulare Grove, on the King's River. It is a fallen trunk, forty-four feet in diameter and one hundred and thirty feet in circumference. In the Fresno Grove, south of the Mariposa, is also a fine collection of these mammoth trees, one of which, still standing, is ninety-six and one-half feet in circumference. The tallest *living* tree of this species now known is said to be located in the Stanislaus Grove, near the sources of the Stanislaus River. It is three hundred and fifty feet high and ninety-seven feet around.

The Calaveras Grove, reached by stage by the way of Stockton and Milton, or from the Narrow Gauge terminus at Valley Springs, through Murphy's, also contains a number of trees possessing special interest to tourists. They are noted for their sky-stabbing propensities — surpassing those of the Mariposa Grove, it is said, both in height and symmetry. It contains, however, only about one hundred trees, the tallest of which is three hundred and twenty-five feet high, though but forty-five feet in circumference. Here it may be well to observe that the relative size of these trees can not be inferred either from their height or circumference. In one instance a tree broken three hundred feet from the ground, was eighteen feet in diameter, even at that extraordinary altitude. There are four trees in all in the Calaveras group now living over three hundred feet high, yet only one of these compares in magnitude with the "Grizzly

KEYSTONE STATE, CALAVERAS GROVE,
325 feet high.

Giant," but two hundred and sixty feet high. Some run to girth, others to grace.

Many of the Calaveras trees have fallen, some of them quite recently. Among these are the "Burnt Tree," three hundred and thirty feet long and ninety-seven feet around, and "The Father of the Forest," four hundred and thirty-five feet in length and one hundred and one feet in circumference. *The largest trees are the fallen.* "Uncle Tom's Cabin" outrivals the "Pioneer's Cabin" of the Mariposa in being capable of comfortably sheltering twenty-five persons who are not over exacting as to elbow room. But the most talked of among the Calaveras trees is the one felled a few years ago by artificial means. How it was overthrown has been a puzzle to many a tourist, and it was not until after many fruitless inquiries that the writer succeeded in getting the mystery solved. It appears that holes were bored into the tree by long pump augurs and the intervening partitions cut away by sawing. So great was the task that five men worked faithfully at the job for more than three weeks, besides spending over two days in driving in wedges to topple it over after the work of cutting through had been finished. This tree, three hundred and two feet high and ninety-six feet in circumference at the ground, was over three thousand years old (as indicated by the annular rings,) and contained half a million cubic feet of lumber, enough to build several incorporated towns. Builders will appreciate these figures. The remaining stump was converted into a dancing platform and the votaries of Terpsichore

IN THE HIGH SIERRAS.

"have measured many a mile to tread a measure" thereon. Within the railing by which it is enclosed four cotillion sets have danced at a time.

These titans of the vegetable world belong to the genus *sequoia*, so called after a half-breed Cherokee chief who invented an Indian alphabet. The species is *gigantœa*, called also *Wellingtonia* by the English botanists and *Washingtonia* by the American. They are closely allied to the redwood, which attains a diameter of sixteen feet and bears the botanical name *sequoia semper virens*. The big trees are often called the "giant redwood," to distinguished them from the common redwood. Both belong to the same family and genus, differing only in species. The former, however, are found only in the Sierras and between the thirty-sixth and thirty-eighth parallels, while the redwood proper, the staple building material of the Pacific Coast, is confined to the coast range.

One by one these monarchs of the forest are yielding to the elements of fire and wind, but there are others of all ages, from saplings up, aspiring to fill their places. So future generations need not borrow trouble for fear they will be cut off from seeing this one of the modern "seven wonders." In view of the fact that these trees are confined to such narrow limits of altitude and latitude, it has often been asked if the species could be reproduced in other localities. I learn from the botanists that it has already been introduced into Great Britain, being there kept on sale in the nurseries; but in the Eastern and Middle States it meets with varying success, being on the whole somewhat hazardous. Still it will stand.

ON THE COAST

Higher up the mountain, beyond the "Big Tree" belt, fir and tamarack pine grow prolific, while below it we found an abundance of pitch and Lambert pine, white cedar and the lofty Douglass spruce. The Lambert—commonly called the sugar-pine—belongs to the sub-genus of white pine and is especially conspicuous along the slopes of the Sierras. It is a remarkable tree and in some places grows to a height of from three hundred to three hundred and fifty feet—thus rivaling in loftiness the Big Trees, though but twelve to fifteen feet in diameter. Its cones are the largest I have ever seen, being from a foot to twenty inches in length and even larger around than they are long.

The supply of available timber in this region, practically inexhaustible, is made accessible by means of long wooden flumes. The one reaching this part of the Sierras has its terminus at Madera on the Southern Pacific Railroad and is fifty-four and one-half miles in length. In 1886 it carried 18,000,000 cubic feet of lumber to the valley. These flumes are sometimes used to convey venturesome passengers down the mountains and the ride is described as being the most exciting imaginable. Mr. H. J. Ramsdell, of the New York *Tribune*, once rode down the Nevada flume in company with the two millionaires—James G. Fair and the late J. C. Flood. They made the entire distance (fifteen miles) in thirty-five minutes, in some parts of the journey going at the rate of nearly a mile a minute. They all barely escaped with their lives, their boats being upset in the passage.

CLIFF HOUSE.

CHAPTER IX.

OBJECTS OF INTEREST IN THE GOLDEN STATE.

Returning to the "Southern Pacific," and thence to San Francisco by rail, we enjoyed a few days of grateful rest in the "Golden Gate" city. San Francisco is noted for its superb hotels, quite as much as for any other single feature of its material make-up. These excel in size and number, as well as beauty of architecture. More people live in hotels here in proportion to the number of inhabitants, than any other city in America. San Francisco is variously called the " City of St. Francis," "Golden Gate City," "Bay City," and "Bay-Window City." To these let us add, "Hotel City." The propriety of this last appellation will not be questioned when it is considered that it has nearly one hundred hotels, over two hundred boarding-houses, two hundred and fifty restaurants and five hundred lodging-houses.

The three principal hotels are the Palace, Grand, and Baldwin, all of which are studded with bay windows on all sides, with a view to meet the popular demand for sunshine. The first two are connected by a corridor over New Montgomery street — both being under the same management. Some idea of the princely character of these hotels may be conceived from the fact that the late Mr. W. C. Ralston spent about seven million dollars in erecting and fitting up

ON WHEELS IN GOLDEN GATE PARK.

the Palace alone. It is a seven-story marble structure, occupying a whole square, the total length of its halls being over three miles. There are three hundred and sixty suites of rooms, about a thousand large single rooms with baths adjoining, and ten spacious dining halls, one of which is one hundred and sixty by fifty-five feet. The hotel has a novel water supply in four artesian wells, situated in the basement, and capable of supplying twenty-five thousand gallons per hour.

Other objects of interest are Golden Gate Park, Nobb Hill — the residence of San Francisco's aristocracy — the Cliff House and Seal Rocks. At the latter place the tourist is sure to be entertained (for a while at least) by the incessant barking and the countless antics of an immense school of seals. These inhabit the rocks called by their name, and situated a few rods off the coast, near the entrance of the Golden Gate. Golden Gate Park, next to Fairmount Park, Philadelphia, is the largest in America. Europe has its equal only in the Bois de Boulogne at Paris. It is three miles long, half a mile wide, with an addition three-quarters of a mile long, extending into the better part of the city. In addition to these lavish dimensions and the elegant drives thus afforded, its attractiveness is greatly enhanced by its half-mile of ocean beach, its two hundred and fifty thousand trees, its imposing conservatory, fine statuary and wild profusion of tropical plants and flowers.

Chinatown is the most novel feature of San Francisco. Visited by night with a policeman or other guide, the tourist is enabled to see "China in a nut-

ALLEY, CHINESE QUARTERS.

shell." Long rows of curiosity shops, the joss houses with their idols and works of Chinese art, the theatres with their clatter and gibberish, the opium hells and underground stables where human beings are huddled together like cattle in a stock-car, all force themselves upon the tourist's sensibilities in this quarter of the city. San Francisco is called the Paris of the Pacific coast. It is not only this, but also the Pekin of America.

The harbor of San Francisco is a veritable wonder. The other night, while crossing the Golden Gate channel, its glory seemed more than ever apparent. Leaving the railroad at Sancelito, we crossed over by steamship just as the sun was setting over the ocean. The crimson rays of this sinking luminary flashing upon the distant heights, Alcatraz bristling with cannon, and the waves glancing in the purple, sun-painted waters, combined with spire and dome and turret looming up from the city, to form a study for the artist and a theme for the poet. The greatest glory of this harbor, however, is the great purpose it so admirably serves. Land-locked, capacious, deep and easily accessible, a more felicitous arrangement for the traffic of the seas could not be well conceived.

Almost every part of the Pacific coast region possesses some peculiar interest to one or another class of tourists. California is replete with mountain, lake and river scenery; it abounds in picturesque cañons and charming valleys; it has a wealth of mines and mineral springs; there are vineyards containing upward of a thousand acres, vast orange groves bending under their burdens of gold, and, in fact, about

"All of beauty and of use,
That one fair country can produce."

Santa Rosa, with its famous Alameda Avenue of willows and enchanting environments, flourishing Fresno, far famed Monterey, the medicinal springs of Paso Robles and Paraiso, the noted saints of the coast, (San Rafael, Santa Cruz, Santa Barbara, Santa Mon-

SAN FRANCISCO BAY.

ica and San Diego), the orange belt of Southern California, Yosemite and the big trees, are all interesting and all conveniently reached by special excursions leading out from San Francisco and Los Angeles.

An interesting and profitable trip from the former of these two pivotal centers of travel is that by the "Southern Pacific" to Marysville, Chico, Red Bluff, Redding and Mount Shasta. This part of the State seems to be coming into greater prominence of late, and really there is much in the way of soil, scenery and climate to give it a claim both upon the tourist and home-seeker. Grain and stock-raising are largely engaged in, but fruit culture is coming rapidly to the front. In Tehama County, of which Red Bluff is the county-seat, are some of the princely posssessions lately owned by the California millionaire, Senator Leland Stanford, but now in the hands of his children. At Vina, a few miles south of Red Bluff, is the famous ranch belonging to this estate, containing fifty-six thousand acres, with its mammoth vineyard, said to be the largest known.

Mount Shasta, the highest mountain of California (fourteen thousand four hundred and forty feet above the sea), has in its vicinity not only some of the grandest scenery of the State, but also the most encouraging field for the sportsman. Here, in addition to the more common game, is the grizzly and black bear, besides deer and other large game, nearly extinct at the south.

But of all the "side trips" from San Francisco, none, save the trip to Yosemite, have so enlisted the writer's enthusiasm as that, one hundred miles north into Lake County, among the hills of the Coast Range. Starting on this trip, we leave San Francisco in the morning. After crossing the bay, we reach Vallejo Junction (pronounced Val-yay-ho) by means of the California Pacific Railroad. Crossing an arm of the bay, called San Pablo, by steamer, we proceeded

VULCAN'S STEAM WORKS.

thence by rail through the delightful, vineyard-studded valley of Napa, reaching the terminus of the iron track at Calistoga in time for dinner. The remaining and most eventful portion of the journey is by stage.

At Calistoga, Senator Stanford once began a series of enterprises for building up a fashionable resort, but abandoned the project in its infancy, leaving here and there only a few scattered reminders of his brilliant conception. On the site of the millionaire's operations are still to be seen the mineral springs that were to work such miraculous healing. Into one or these I carelessly thrust my hand to determine the temperature but was summarily reminded of the indiscretion. These springs are said to be turned to practical use by the bland Chinaman, who finds them admirably adapted for scalding his hogs and chickens. The service which they have performed in this direction has given them the characteristic flavor of pork and chicken soup — so our guide informed us.

A few miles from here the demon of fire has evidently a still more approved heating apparatus, since, at a place known as the "Geysers," the earth boils and bubbles all around you, horrid sounds and suggestive odors fill the air, while seething caldrons and the shrill whistle of escaping steam add to the accumulating testimony that you are paying a visit to the "Devil's Workshop." Here, too, is the "Devil's Inkstand," the "Devil's Pulpit," and other property supposed to belong to the proprietor of the bottomless pit.

A few miles' drive from Calistoga also brings us to the "Petrified Forest." Huge trunks of fallen trees

THE PETRIFIED FOREST.

are here exposed to view in a perfect state of petrifaction. Most of them have so preserved their original form and appearance that the deception is detected only by close inspection. Our guide, with much display of emotion, pointed out a small block lying on the bank which a callow youth from Boston recently tried to kick out of his path. The tale which all coming generations of tourists to this place will hear concerning the yawning boot and shattered phalanges of this Boston youth will doubtless prove a sufficient warning against the danger of trifling with the fateful delusions. At the entrance of the Petrified Forest is a spring of arsenic water. This the tourist is expected to sample, if for no other reason, to gratify the officious guide, who manifests a commendable anxiety to return a full equivalent for the price of admission to the grove. The effect of this water is seen in the alabaster complexion of some of the neighboring people who are addicted to its use. A lady here died from its effects some time ago. Still they *will* use it. "Beautiful or bust" seems to be the motto. After securing some desirable specimens we returned to Calistoga, catching here and there glimpses of pleasing scenes en route.

After two days of rest and entertainment in the vicinity of Calistoga, we proceeded by Wellington's line of six-horse coaches over one of the most romantic drives of the State to the lake region. This fifty-mile trip over the Coast Hills is considered one of the very best examples of mountain staging in the country. One who is accustomed to nothing more than an or-

THE DEVIL'S CAÑON.

dinary drive in his easy chaise can scarcely conceive the real nature of this exciting ride over hills and mountains. The fore part of the journey is unmistakably uphill, but when the summits of Cobb and St. Helena mountains are reached the general grade seems downward.

Beyond these summits we cover the highway at a dashing rate. On we go by a series of curves, ups and downs, right-angles and straight shoots through the air,

At one time we seem to be going up one side of a mammoth hencoop and down the other. What feats our imaginations tell us we are performing! Now comes the sensation of riding over the arc of a semi-circle on its hollow side. Next we make the same excursion over the convex rim of the semi-circle inverted. Wonder follows wonder. We continue to experiment with the semi-circle until we think we have made its detour in every conceivable position. Then we take up the complete circle until, finally, by a master stroke, we make the entire circumference heels over head half the way round. It may be asked how we managed not to spill out of the coach while it was bottom side upward; but we did not pretend to rely upon gravity at any time to keep our positions. A precipitous bank at one point in the journey appears directly in front of us—we are shooting like an arrow toward it—what can possibly restrain us from plunging headlong into the deep abyss? At this crisis a woman sitting on the same seat with the driver begins to scream and grasps at the lines. But the cool-headed pilot of our destiny keeps a firm hold on the reins and steers us aside unharmed.

But behold! what next? All at once we encounter a field of glass—glass pebbles—glass stones—glass boulders. What means the reckless distribution of so valuable an article of commerce? The driver relieves the puzzled tourists of further suspense by breaking the news that we are in the midst of a volcanic region. Being assured that the volcanoes are all extinct and harmless we breathe easy. We are now nearing our

OBJECTS OF INTEREST. 147

ROUGH BUT ROMANTIC

destination. This obsidian, locally known as "bottle-glass," continues to strew the earth along the way. Chaparral-crowned hills and grassy lawns, studded with oak, rise up before us in rapid succession. Here and there the white petals of the azalea are seen flapping their liliputian banners in the sunlight, while moss and mistletoe hang luxuriant from hoary pines. The glaring "red-bud," like a burning bush, shoots out from the thicket and blossoms of crimson and gold flame with beauty along the roadside. The eye is constantly refreshed by changing scenes, new vistas of charming scenery appear and disappear—there is nothing tame or trashy in a drive like this. But now we have come to a more level region; the road-bed begins to assume a more consistent trend and we glide smoothly along the shores of Clear Lake. Taking supper at Kelseyville, we reach Lakeport just at night-fall, there consigning to the arms of Morpheus all that remains of our mortal baggage.

From Lakeport we proceeded the next day to Blue Lakes, "Saratoga Springs" and other points of interest. The whole region is most delectable. The air is bracing, the climate healthful and the scenery commanding and noble. All about the country are numberless mineral springs, where iron, sulphur and soda, and in fact nearly all the elements combined in favorite proportions, pour from nature's great soda fountain according to her clever caprice. In these fascinating environments, among these romantic hills, and on the shores of these beautiful mountain lakes we spent three weeks and over in a state of blissful satisfaction. Rowing, sailing and fishing on the lakes and deer hunting on the mountains were our chief occupations. These we carried on with success, and were it not for the consideration that deer and fish stories are little esteemed and seldom believed, I would be tempted to recount some of our thrilling adventures with rod and gun.

CHAPTER X.

THE CLIMATE OF CALIFORNIA.

From the time Helen Hunt Jackson wrote her famous articles to "The Century," to the present moment, poets, novelists, landlords and real-estate agents have sung the praises of Southern California. Medical authorities, too, of good repute, have accorded it a high place among the world's noted sanitaria. John Muir, the writer, referring to the banner valley of Southern California — the San Gabriel — says:

"It is one of the brightest spots in all our fair land and most of its brightness is wildness — wild south sunshine in a basin rimmed about with mountains." Dr. Congar, a resident physician, says of this valley:

"The geographical position is exactly right, soil and climate perfect, and everything that heart can wish comes for our efforts — flowers, fruits, milk and honey, and plenty of money." Dr. Chamberlain of Charity Hospital, New York, a more disinterested authority, says:

"The long, bright days of Southern California, with unclouded sky, mild and even warmth and gentle winds, invite the invalid to live in open air and protects him while there."

Dr. Lindley of the "Southern California University," vouches that he has "never known a child born in Southern California of a phthisical parent to die of pulmonary disease. This is a paradise," he adds "for persons who have passed the meridian of life. Instead of spending most of their lives in rooms artificially heated, they get a new lease of life from the sun's rays, the pure atmosphere and inspiring surroundings."

One of the great advantages of this southern climate is alleged to be the *small difference* between the mean temperature of the *coldest* and *warmest* parts of the year. For example: The difference between the mean temperature of January and July in New York is forty-six degrees, while this difference at Los Angeles is but eighteen degrees, at San Diego eight, Santa Monica seven, and Monterey six, the last three places being on the coast. These differences are indeed a marked contrast with those of Eastern cities, which, like Washington and St. Paul, hold their warm and cold months far apart, this difference being in the case of these two cities forty and fifty-seven degrees respectively. The Los Angeles signal service records show that, for six years, the coldest month of the year has an average temperature of fifty-two degrees and the warmest month about seventy degrees.

This feature, so much dwelt upon by the zealous climatist, is plausible and worthy of due estimation by those seeking a more beneficent sky; but there are other facts and considerations which must be kept in mind — qualifying as they do this theory of *uniform* temperature. It will be noticed that these places hav-

FRUIT SCENE IN SOUTHERN CALIFORNIA.

ing such uniformity are, with the exception of Los Angeles, on the coast, and the latter is but eighteen miles inland. If it be desirable for people with disordered lungs to live on or near the coast, then this theory of uniform temperature is especially pertinent. But as we move landward toward the interior valleys, this gulf between the warmest and coldest parts of the year materially widens. It is difficult to get statistics on the subject, since the records in these newer settlements, away from the direct ocean winds are limited or else entirely wanting. Besides, weather statistics are somewhat misleading in California, since, on account of the wide daily range of the thermometer, extremes in part offset each other, some portion of an excessively hot day usually having an opposite excess of cold, which puts the day on record as one of moderate temperature, and secures a fair showing for the monthly average. We can also easily reason from analogy that this uniformity does not prevail in any such degree in the interior. The short distance of eighteen miles recession makes a difference of ten degrees or more in the case of Los Angeles, and a considerable greater difference must maintain in the valleys still further removed from the tempering influence of the trade winds. Adding to this the results of inland observations, personal experience, and the testimony of friends having longer periods of observation upon which to base opinion, and the necessary conclusion is reached that this uniformity of temperature in the interior is not so remarkable, but that the climate is at times continuously and exces-

TROPIC FOLIAGE, COAST.

sively *hot*. The *debilitating* effect of this condition can not be questioned. It made itself apparent as applied to those coming under my own observation as early as the month of March and was much commented upon by Eastern tourists. I find similar reports of other years — reports given by those who had no climatic investments at stake and no interest in conveying false impressions of the country.

The winters of Southern California are, without question, delightfully mild, and this seems to be its distinctive merit. Still there are others, who view the subject in a different light, refusing to recalcitrate against the *exceeding* mildness of the warmer months. This is the case with some permanent residents, who accept, in much the same spirit, the matchless glory of flowery winter and what the writer viewed as the sardonic and vituperable " mildness " of recreant summer.

The thermometer, skirmishing recklessly about among the nineties in the shade, and that too for many days in succession and as early as the month of March, as the writer has known to be the case, must at least modify some of the utopian representations of Southern California's faultless climate. The effect of this excessive heat was observed to be depressing to invalids and seriously prejudicial to their progress.

In the San Joaquin Valley, I found the heat even *more* oppressive than at the same time of year at the South. The reason for this is easily understood. The ocean winds (known among climatologists as the polar currents) in sweeping southward over Oregon and Northern California become more and more dessicated

RESIDENCE MONTECITO, COAST

of moisture as they advance over the dry soil of these regions. By the time they reach the San Joaquin Valley, they have become almost completely deprived of moisture and heated to a high degree by contact with the plains. These hot winds from the north, however, being obstructed by the Tehachepi mountains or else meeting counter-currents from the south do not often affect the southern part of the state. They seem content to let loose their fury in the larger valleys at the north. Nothing therefore is gained in the way of comfort or benefit by emigrating to the plains beyond the Tehachepi mountains.

The one dominating incentive of this chapter being the desire to present truthful information concerning the climate of California, for the benefit of tourists and climate-seekers from the East who are every year resorting hither, it will, I trust, be profitable to enter a little more into detail and sum up briefly and impartially as possible the results of the writer's investigation of this subject.

First as regards the coast. Here, for causes well understood, the temperature is notably uniform; but this uniformity does not necessarily make it the paragon of resorts for the lung invalid. Nature, indeed, never leaves all her treasures in one place. Whenever there is a marked difference between the temperature of the Japan current (which skirts the coast of California) and the surrounding ocean, or when the northerly and southerly winds interlace their unequal temperatures, the result is seen in the vast volumes of fog which blow in upon the coast. In the spring these

WOODARD'S GARDENS, GOLDEN GATE.

fogs prevail nearly throughout the length of the state, while at San Francisco and other places north, they continue during the summer. The greater part of the coast country is, in fact, subject to them nearly three-fourths of the year. But even when these do not prevail, the air is much of the time charged with an excess of moisture. The average humidity, for the year, on the coast is seventy per cent., while sixty per cent. is the normal, and for diseased lungs a less degree than this is generally recommended. Hence, since fog is not produced till the air reaches one hundred per cent. humidity, it will be readily seen that, in the absence of fog, this excess of moisture may prove very prejudicial to the invalid—especially such as are afflicted with asthma or consumption, for the relief of which dry air is indispensable. It may be well to observe, however, that Santa Barbara and Monterey, shielded as they are from the direct ocean winds by projecting headlands, and San Diego spared from fog by the recession of the Japan current, are held in much esteem as coast resorts. The southern coast is in fact less afflicted with a humid atmosphere than the northern. It seems, indeed, specially agreeable and beneficial to some constitutions, while to others it is positively hazardous—personal idiosyncrasies doubtless accounting for these discordant results. Persons having a predilection for the seaside can easily visit some of the favored resorts of the coast and test their virtues as applied to the case in hand. In general, the humidity diminishes about one per cent. to every five miles recession to the eastward; and thus it may be roughly (and quite roughly) estimated how far inland the patient, sensitive to moist air, will find it advisable to locate.

Now let us revert to the north and make a few wholesome comparisons. That the climate of Northern California has been the victim of many popular misapprehensions it is eminently safe to assert. There is, indeed, a current notion that Northern and Southern California are distinct entities—the one an insalubrious region of extreme heat and cold—the other a blooming paradise of tropical fruits and unfailing health.

There is a cause for this false view. Those who come to California in the winter (and most of the immigration thither is at that season) are in many cases impelled to steer toward the warmer zone and hence take the southern routes, visiting Los Angeles and vicinity first. Here a persistent effort is made to convince the tourist that throughout the north adverse elements prevail and that the only Elysium is Southern California. As an illustration of this spirit to decry the north and extol the south, a citizen of Pasadena was one day vehemently setting forth to me the various objections to the climate of a certain northern city—berating it *ad extremum*. Accepting his representations, I logically and innocently asked, if he thought I would take many chances on my life, in breathing the air there, should I stop off between trains to see the town. Thereupon he suddenly turned the topic of conversation while bystanders, as summarily retired, their handkerchiefs, at the same time vigorously wrestling with the intractible muscles of the face. Notwithstanding this stampede I persisted in having my enquiry answered, insisting that it was exactly to the point. But for some reason I couldn't make him see it in that light, as he had now got his mind on the oat crops.

The average Southern Calfornian, gradually catching up the spirit and phraseology of the lucre-aspiring *confreres* of Autolycus, would have the Eastern tourist believe that a "Mason and Dixon's line" of climate separates Northern and Southern California. This is by no means true of all, but notably of those who spend much time within hearing-distance of the "boomers" or within reading-range of hotel and real estate literature.

As a matter of fact, from the parallel of San Diego, within two hours drive of Mexico, to that of Mt. Shasta, near the Oregon line, the same general characteristics of climate prevail. Great differences indeed exist along the parallels and almost any desired climate may be had by traveling due eastward from the coast. But moving north and south along the meridians, it would puzzle the most acute observer from abroad to state within three or four hundred miles where our good southern friends would draw the climate-line between the Eldorado of sunshine and the "inhospitable" North. The mean annual temperature along the coast is the same for more than five hundred miles, while the mean *summer* temperature in this belt is the same for over *eight hundred* miles; in fact greater differences of climate are often encountered in a single

NAPA SODA SPRINGS, ORANGE AND VINE CULTURE, NORTHERN CALIFORNIA.

day's drive from the coast eastward, than exist at the same time between Los Angeles and Puget's Sound,— a thousand miles apart.

So, in the *interior*, the same *general* characteristics prevail throughout the state. The mean annual temperature at Redding, in the northern part of the Sacramento Valley, is almost precisely the same as that at Tulare in the southern part of the San Joaquin. The mean annual temperature of Sacramento, the coolest place in the Sacramento Valley, is the same as that of Los Angeles, the coolest city in the valleys of Southern California. The great interior plains of the north have likewise no monopoly in summer heat. The same, somewhat mitigated, is incident to the south as well.

Other features in common are equally suggestive. One of these is found in the circumstance that the north is presenting the same stages of development already witnessed at the south — illustrating the common character of their climate and resources in a striking manner. In the early times we find Southern California given over to the dominant occupation of stock raising. Then followed the more profitable era of agriculture ; next the cultivation of tropical fruits ; and lastly, the cultivation of Quixotic prices — the latter being based upon the alleged value created by superior climatic advantages for the invalid and homeseeker. These same evolutions are to-day unquestionably in progress at the north. The era of horticulture has for years been crowding close upon that of grazing and agriculture, and already the three industries are unmistakably wedded. The recent pomological dis-

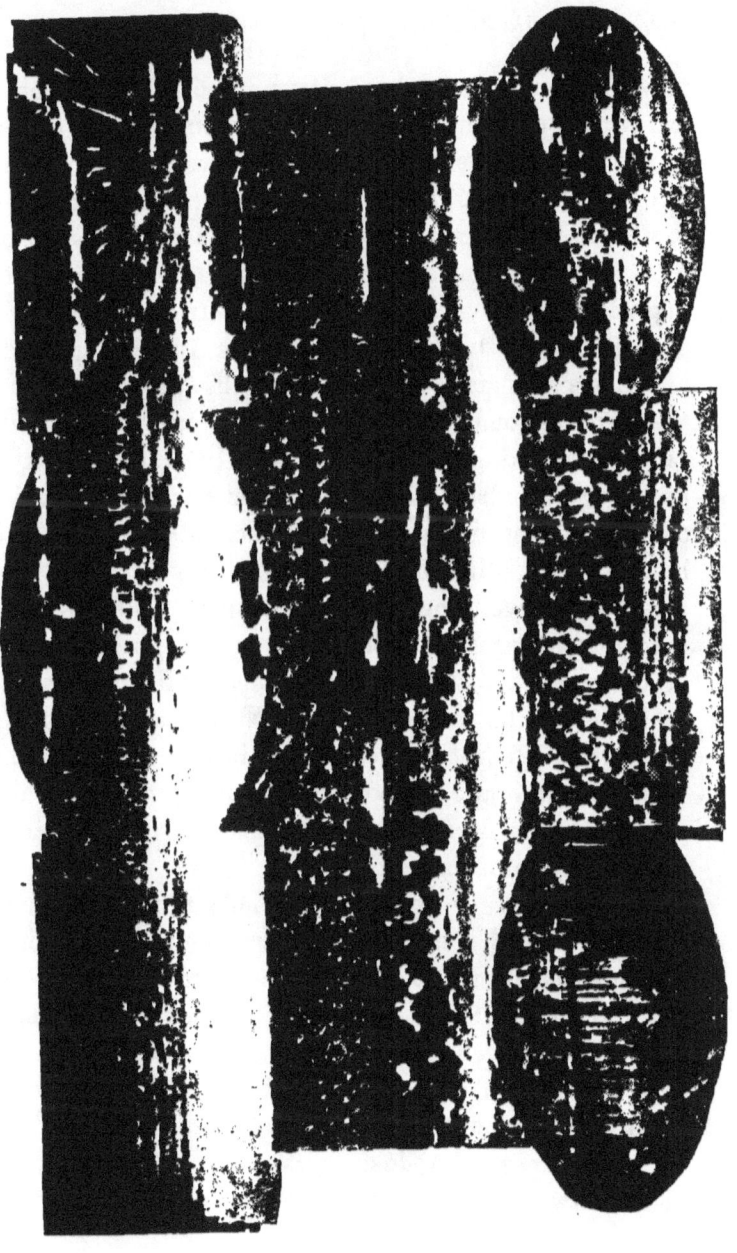

FRUIT RANCHES, NORTHERN CALIFORNIA.

plays, in which all kinds of citrus and other semi-tropical fruits grown at the north, were exhibited, have sufficiently evinced the horticultural resources of Northern California. Indeed the north has some advantages over the south in this respect, being able to largely dispense with irrigation and favored with the great center of population conveniently accessible. In nearly all the counties along the Sacramento River the orange and lemon are in a state of profitable cultivation, and even the olive, almond, fig, persimmon, English walnut and raisin are making rapid headway. In Butte County, nearly two hundred miles north from San Francisco, is one of the best citrus regions in the state ; and in Tehama County, still further north, the largest, if not the most productive, vineyard in the world. Indeed there is scarcely a species of fruit of commanding importance at the south that is not being sucessfully cultivated in the foot-hills and valleys of Northern California. Some varieties succeed even better in the latter region. These considerations show the manifest absurdity of the distinction, in the accepted sense, of Northern and Southern California.

As a retreat for invalids, especially those suffering from pulmonary complaints, without doubt more comfort and benefit are realized, in the warmer months, in the northerly portions of the state. But here as elsewhere the convalescent must exercise judgment. It would hardly be advisable, at least during the summer months, to take up quarters on the plains of either the Sacramento or San Joaquin Valley. On the other hand, notwithstanding there are those who delight in pitching their fortunes high up among the snows of the Sierras, it is doubtful if the health-seeker should locate much if any above the line of four thousand feet equal elevation — the line drawn by topographers between the *secondary* foot-hills and the great timber belt of the Sierras.

But between these extremes of heat and cold — the low plains and the high Sierras — may be found — not the superb hotels of less deserving resorts — but dry bracing breezes freighted with health and healing. The whole country embraced between the alluvial lands of the valleys and the line of four thousand feet elevation just referred to, a territory at least twenty thousand square miles in area, is a region possessing remarkable sanative properties for the relief of pulmonary troubles. In the western foot-hills of the Coast Range similar conditions are also to be found — in either region the *primary* foot-hills (below the line of two thousand feet elevation) being perhaps most desirable for the average invalid.

It should here be observed that the foot-hills and valleys of the Sierras and Coast Range possess a variety of climatic conditions, owing to peculiar configurations in the mountains, the proximity of snow-capped peaks and the course of the winds. In the region of the "Thermal Belt" however, the climate seeker is reasonably secure from adverse influences. This thermal belt is a warm zone existing at a moderate altitude and nearly surrounding the great interior valley.

It is also here in place to note the fact that no climate is to be found on the Pacific coast that can promise much to those in the *advanced* stages of consumption. But those upon whom the disease is not deeply rooted find great relief and often complete recovery. There is nothing inherent in the atmosphere, as some would seem to infer, that is proof against troubles of a phthisical nature. The native white population indeed enjoys remarkable immunity from these afflictions, but investigation shows that among the native Spaniards, lung diseases (especially consumption) are very common and yearly on the increase. But this strange inconsistency is not allowed to go unexplained. Close inter-marriages, sudden change in mode of life since the supremacy of the white population, and the depraved and wretched condition in which the average native lives, are the alleged causes of these startling developments. Still this straw points to an important factor among the remedial influences which add celebrity to health-resorts and at the same time furnishes a timely and suggestive hint of much value to the convalescent. It shows the paramount importance of looking well to other conditions as well as those of climate. The locality, the temperature and elevation may all be right, but if other sanitary precautions are ignored, these are of little avail. The luxurious winters of Southern California; the three hundred days of coveted sunshine which bless the year in almost every part of the State; the recruiting winds that fan the valleys and hill-sides — these are all futile in the absence of personal care. This care should be exercised in making the immediate surroundings wholesome and inviting, wearing suitable apparal, avoid-

HAUNTS OF THE TROUT.

ing exposure to damp air and chilling winds ; in locating, if possible, apart from those having kindred ailments, securing well-prepared and palatable food, pleasant scenery, cheerful associations and an open air life. To these should be added, agreeable employment, judicious recreation with horse and rod and gun, or, indeed, any well-chosen means of exercise conducive to normal appetite, free respiration and a contented frame of mind. In the pacific and antiseptic air of this western coast, thus supplemented by these and similar precautions and expedients, there is undoubted virtue. The patient over whom the wasting disease has not gained ascendancy has many reasons for entertaining good cheer and hope, and confidently looking forward to renewed health and happiness.

CHAPTER XI.

THE CITY OF THE SAINTS.

After so long and delightful a sojourn in the sunny land of Proteus, it was with somewhat of reluctance that we entertained the thought of leaving the scene of so many pleasing and inspiring associations. But even the gods do not always hover about Olympus, and so in our case it seemed advisable to break loose from these attractions and this novel paradise to which Uncle Sam holds title on the Pacific Coast.

Leaving San Francisco by the way of the Central Pacific, we passed through the productive valley of the Sacramento to the capital city, whence, after a brief stop, we proceeded to climb the Sierras on the iron rail, and soon found ourselves at Auburn, a charming village among the foothills. The first verse of Goldsmith's "Village," slightly paraphrased, admirably applies to this place — it being only necessary to substitute the word "foothills" for "plain." Here we laid over one day, taking the sleeper the following night *en route* for Ogden and the Salt Lake region.

It seemed a pity to ride over the Sierras by night, and thus be deprived of seeing the wild and rugged scenery which friends and guide-books informed us to be highly interesting; but we were in part consoled by the reflection that we had already enjoyed more than an average dose of mountain wonders, and fell to sleep in good conscience. Our night journey took us by the famous mountain pass, "Cape Horn," where it is said the passenger is able, by extending his arm from the window, to drop a stone half a mile perpendicular into the cañon below. But we rode over those frightful precipices and terrifying chasms without rigidity of the scalp or an extra thump of the heart.

In this night journey we also passed near by the celebrated lakes on the summit of the Sierras — Lake Tahoe, Donner and Webber — resorts much frequented and possessing, it is said, fine scenic attractions. These places are reached by short side tracks from the main line, being easily accessible. Not having personally visited them, the best I can do is to give the reader a panoramic view of these novel sheets of water high up in the firmament.

After breakfasting at Reno, a town of over four thousand inhabitants just over the line in Nevada and the gateway to the famous Comstock mines, we speeded eastward through the great Nevada desert. This appeals to every sense as an abandoned and desolate region — nothing in the form of vegetable life cheering the eye, except the artemisia or sage-bush, and nothing in the animal kingdom but lizards and jack-rabbits.

The nomenclature of this region is quite descriptive — "Desert," "Hot Springs," "Mirage," "White Plains," "Winnemucca," "Piute," and other station names equally novel but with applications less apparent. The prepossession, more and more confirmed, that we are in a land of desolation without agricultural

THE STATE CAPITOL

possibilities, is modified by the cheering oasis at Humboldt, the dinner station, and especially by the phenomena which, after a ride of thirty hours through the forbidding country, presents itself in the fertile valley of the Mormons.

After a short lay-off at Ogden, which was made still shorter by the satisfying employment of reinstating the inner man, made sensibly vacuitous by the desert ride, we transferred to the "scenic route" — the Denver & Rio Grande — and are soon brought to the world-renowned "City of the Saints."

In the way of natural scenery there are many objects of interest in the vicinity of Salt Lake City, prominent among which is the great Salt Lake itself — a sheet of such notoriety that one would scarcely wish to pass it without examining its peculiar saline and anti-sinking properties. This we visited several times, daily excursions making it conveniently accessible by rail, a distance of thirteen miles from the city. It was, however, rather too cold for comfort, the best time for bathing being in July and August.

North of the city the Mount of Prophecy, which towers with dignified grace, furnishes the best lookout upon the valley. From its oval summit the observer looks down upon the silvery waters of the Dead Sea at the west, and below, at the south, sees the City of the Saints and the beautiful valley of Jordon. The latter is hemmed in by the Oquirrh Mountains on the west, and the Wasatch on the east, altogether presenting a picture of true sublimity. At the east also there is an opening in the mountains, and in this direction Camp

OVER THE SIERRA SUMMITS,

Douglass, happily situated on a bench at the base of the mountain, overlooks the city. Below this camp is the famous Emigration Cañon, threading its way between the mountains. This is historic ground, being the place where Brigham Young and the "Pioneer Band" entered the valley, and in fact the beaten track through which the long train of emigrant turnouts filed their way westward in the early days. A history of those times that did not recount the sentimental events occurring in this cañon would indeed be a *rara avis* of its kind.

Close by is Parley's Cañon and Parley's Park. These places are so named from Parley Pratt, a zealous Mormon, who had six wives besides Mrs. Hector McLean, whom he converted and with whom he absconded. For his greed on this occasion he received his reward in this world by being carved into sliced bacon with a bowie knife wielded by the enraged husband, and in the next by being enrolled among the "Glorious Martyrs" to the Mormon faith.

Beyond this park, to the south, are a succession of interesting places — South Mill Creek and Cottonwood Cañon, Silver Mountain, the well-known Flag-staff, North Star and Emma Mines, and, still further on, grand old Mount Nebo, twelve thousand feet high.

Weber, Echo and American Fork cañons are all in the vicinity and noted places of interest easily reached.

More than a decade and a half ago an observant American writer said, "Ten years hence, scarcely a relic of polygamy and the patriarchal system will

LAKE ESTHER, SIERRA NEVADA MOUNTAINS.

remain." The fulfillment of this bold prophecy surely can not be claimed, and especially when made to apply to the visible institutions of this polygamous order of saints. For it is their works that to-day astonish the stranger who, for leagues away, espies the mysterious prodigies of their architectural skill looming up in the midst of a desert country, as if called into being by a Druid's wand. These imposing edifices overtop the city itself in most suggestive proportions, dispelling all doubt as to relics of the patriarchal system.

Proceeding to make a closer inspection of the remarkable structures which so rivited our attention in the distance, and which we found mainly located in Temple Block, in a prominent part of the city, we were at once confronted by a mammoth temple, old in story but new in aspect. This has already been in process of erection for over thirty-five years, and though still not complete, has nearly reached the designed height of ninety-nine feet. Its massive walls are from seven to nine feet thick, and are composed of solid granite of a superior quality, hewn out of the neighboring mountains. The Temple is intended for the mystic rites now performed in the Endowment House, and not for regular public service. The outside world must therefore be content to regale the senses upon its external beauty, blissfully ignorant of the Elusinian mysteries within.

The windows are very peculiar, those of the second and fourth stories being circular and the keystone over each having a star set in bold relief. Circular bosses on the sides are adorned with suns, moons and stars,

LAKE DONNER.

and, it is said, maps of the world are to be added in other places. The cost of the building, by the most conservative calculation, has already reached two million dollars, while estimates run from this up to fifteen millions; but such matters are usually overdrawn. Probably at least another million will be required for its completion, although work appears at present to be practically suspended.

Close by in Temple Block is a clumsy, but very impressive structure two hundred and fifty feet long by one hundred and fifty wide. This is the Tabernacle. It holds aloft an immense roof, resembling (as the janitor informed us) a vast boat turned bottom side up. This roof is supported by forty-six pillars of red cut sandstone, six feet square, ten feet high, and extending around the whole building. In the centre the roof is sixty-five feet above the floor. The janitor showed us its wonderful acoustic properties by dropping a pin at one end of the building, while the company remained at the other, the sound being distinctly heard by all. It is said, however, that between these points sounds become so blended that hearing is not such a luxury as might be inferred from the success of this experiment.

The great organ, we were told by the guide, has twenty-eight hundred pipes and fifty-seven stops. It is forty-eight feet high, thirty-six deep, thirty-three wide, and alleged to be next to the largest in America. The Tabernacle seats ten thousand, while thirteen thousand have been accommodated. In front of the organ and the rostrum are three descending seats, the

LAKE TAHOE.

upper having been formerly occupied by Brigham Young, the next by apostles, and the lower by high priests.

The Endowment House, concerning the mysteries of which there has been so much speculation, is situated in Temple Block, northwest of the new Tabernacle, being located in the same quarter of the block with the old Tabernacle.

Assembly Hall, a more modern structure, with minarets tastefully adorning the outer edges of its roof, is just south of the Tabernacle, and furnishes a very convenient building for the transaction of business and the holding of meetings not largely attended. Its inside walls are elaborately illustrated with scenes of Mormon history and achievement.

Leaving Temple Block by the south exit, through a turreted adobe wall twelve feet high, we find ourselves on South Temple street, a noted Mormon avenue. Passing a few rods eastward we cross East Temple street and come to Prophets' Block, directly east of Temple Block. At the nearest corner is an antiquated building which constituted the old Mormon store, and is now devoted to the "Deseret News" and other Mormon publications. East of this is the Tithing House and Court, and a little further on the Lion and Bee-hive houses, where Brigham Young managed his conclave of concubines. Over the Bee-hive House is an emblematic bee-hive carved in stone. Some have interpreted this as symbolic of the annual swarming of progeny, but inquiry quickly dispels the

SCENES IN THE NEVADA DESERT.

hallucination, as it will be promptly explained as typifying industry.

Eagle Gate, just east of the Bee-hive, is a name applied to the entrance to City Creek Cañon, which is reached by passing under an immense arch surmounted by an eagle, carved in wood. This cañon furnishes the source of water supply for the city. Just north of these hot-beds of polygamy is the Kimball Block, the premises consisting of one large dwelling and several smaller ones, once owned by the late Heber C. Kimball, of Mormon fame, who had seventeen wives. Just across the way from the Bee-hive is the Amelia Palace, named in honor of Brigham's favorite Amelia. This was for a long time the finest residence between the Pacific coast and the Missouri River.

Zion's Co-operative Mercantile Institute, the name applied to the present Mormon store, is a really creditable building, combining beauty and utility in a degree seldom attained in Mormon architecture.

Salt Lake City is about four thousand, three hundred feet above sea level and was laid out in 1847, just before the gold excitement in California. Each street is one hundred and thirty-two feet wide, each block forty rods square, containing ten acres each. There are nine squares to each ward. Many of the buildings are of adobe brick. The yards are well kept, most of them being decorated with various kinds of shrubbery, trees and flowers.

To one riding through long stretches of the desert region, the sight of green vegetation, fruitful orchards, floral lawns and tasty dwellings can scarcely fail to

"HOSTILE ELEMENTS."

awaken emotion and elicit praise, if not applause—
these cheerful manifestations so strangely contrasting
with the desolate solitudes in such close proximity.
Even more must this have been the case in early times
when the overland immigrant, after weeks and months
of weary travel through arid desert and rugged cañon,
constantly menaced by the savagery of man and
beast and the hostile elements of nature, first
caught sight of this cheering oasis in his restless
march to the interior. For nearly a quarter of a century
Salt Lake City was the only place of importance between the Mississippi Valley and the Pacific Slope—
practically the only relief station on the way. Its
streets aligned with refreshing streams of running
water, its verdant lawns and neat cottages, its weird
scenery of mountain and plain, its mysterious religious
atmosphere and peculiar people — these, in connection
with the peculiar frame of mind in which the average
immigrant approached its borders, have seldom failed to
invest the region with something more than a tinsel
of enchantment.

One thing was especially impressive to the writer
and that was the orderly conduct of the inhabitants
and the commendable business-like manner which pre-
vailed. The signs of culture, however, are not so
marked, while the average female is not conspicuously
prepossessing. The children are orderly on the street,
and very reticent as to all matters pertaining to their
religion. "I don't know" is the stereotyped reply, at
times accompanied by a significant twinkle of the eye
which says: "I *do* know all the same, but you are

not going to get any tales from me." We did not, indeed, obtain but one really instructive piece of information from the rising generation, and that was from a bright boy of twelve summers, who, in response to our enquiries replied with a glow of sentiment: "Brigham Young was my grandfather, but he was an awful scoundrel."

CHAPTER XII.

IN PURSUIT OF KNOWLEDGE.

The visitor who tarries at Salt Lake City for any considerable length of time discovers upon close observation and careful study, a dual condition. The one phase is so unlike the other, he is almost persuaded that two distinct cities occupy the same ground. The exterior one is the pride of both citizen and tourist. Of the other we will speak with caution; still it exists and for convenience might be called *indoor* as distinguished from *outdoor* Mormondom. Very few tourists, owing to the difficulties and uncertainties attending the undertaking, enter its forbidding labyrinths. They are as a rule content to view the mammoth buildings of "the saints," watch the flowing streams that bound their broad avenues, or regale the senses upon the sweet odors of their floral gardens; but to enter the precincts of the less material city within, and study its make-up, there seems little disposition. But to the writer the indoor exhibition has proved quite as interesting if not so meritorious.

The reader may infer that I have been exploring the mysteries of the "Endowment house" and the Freemasonry of Mormonism. Nothing of the kind; but rather the more vital mysteries of their creed and its influence on social and domestic life. Despite the perplexities of the undertaking it seemed desirable to catch a glimpse, if possible, of the inspiring and controlling forces behind the fair outside and learn something of indoor Mormonism. Surely such a great institution with such colossal and costly structures, attractive exteriors and magnificent environments must have some grand purpose or high mission—some great truth or sublime thought—to offer. This was what I was anxious to study—the intellectual animus—the mode of thinking—the highest thought—in a word the soul of Mormonism. Without detailing the difficulties in the way of one's efforts to probe for the supposed treasure, it is sufficient to say that no opportunity was neglected to interview dignitaries of the church of "The Saints," in order to get at the true inwardness of the Mormon theocracy and the source of its inspiration.

The first officer interviewed was freely communicative and fully prepared to unfold the history and doctrines of the sect, but unfortunately so entirely averse to hearing anyone talk but himself that questions received but scant consideration. This first tedious and profitless interview was supplemented by others equally fruitless, so far as concerned the end desired. Yet all might be considered instructive as presenting different phases of Mormon character and showing up the mental calibre of the Mormon hierarchy, in neither of which was anything specially refreshing to be detected, unless it were a certain passing civility and plausible manner of discourse. Recent events have seemed to make Mormons unusually suspicious. Having accomplished nothing to the purpose thus far, it occurred to me that I had better try one of the Evangelists, of whose whereabouts I had been apprised, knowing that if I posed as a seeker for light his peculiar mission would necessitate a considerate regard for my enquiries, especially if presented in the form of doubts and perplexities. I had, therefore, renewed confidence in my enterprise and with good courage called at his place. Here I was welcomed by a really creditable representative of his order, judging from appearances. After certain preliminary conversation, in which I was careful to preserve the mood of one in sympathy with his surroundings, I observed: "Now, Mr. R——, you have, without doubt, already detected that I am a Gentile, and somewhat in the dark as to your doctrines and practices. Being a reverent searcher after truth, I feel special interest in this subject, and have a great desire to know more about Mormonism."

In a tone and manner indicating that he was at my service, the evangelist, who seemed to be fully loaded for the occasion, replied:

"My dear sir, I can fully appreciate your attitude. It is just what mine was before I became connected with the Mormon Church. I never condemed anything without a hearing, and was always open to conviction. I have been a protestant, a Catholic, an infidel, and, lastly, a Mormon; and even to-day, if you can show me that science, philosophy, reason, common-sense and inspiration are not all in support of Mormonism, I will renounce it."

"But, Mr. R——, you understand I am not here to convert you to any other creed, but to be enlightened."

BIRD'S-EYE VIEW OF SALT LAKE CITY

Evangelist: "Yes, I see; everything indicates this, and I heartily commend the attitude you take. Well, I will say Mormonism is the exponent of all wisdom. Nothing ever was or can be known, more than Mormonism teaches. It embraces all of past and all of future knowledge. It is a complete system of morality, of religion, science, ethics and philosophy, and embraces all of wisdom past and future, known or knowable."

Disciple: "Well, if that's so, I have no objections to Mormonism; you may safely count on another convert. A religion that embraces those features is good enough for me."

Evangelist: "Yes, and I will go further (lighting up with new enthusiasm); if you can show me anything in the Scriptures that is anti-Mormon, or that I can not show to be consistent with or explainable by our creed, I will also renounce my faith."

Disciple: "I declare! that's strange language. It really looks as if you Mormons were on the right track."

Evangelist: "Why! I know we are. Scripture says: 'Ye shall know' — have positive assurance — and this we claim to have. Take, for example, even the question of plural marriage, over which Christians have raised such a hullaballoo: While the Old and the New Testaments do not deal specifically with the matter, what *is* said is, on the whole, in favor of the system. As Mr. Stillman said, a few years ago, in Boston [at the same time pointing out the passage in a Mormon tract which lay on the table and which he requested me to keep]: ' There is not a single precept in the book known as the Holy Bible, supposed by Christians to be the inspired word of God and the

SEEKING INFORMATION.

rule of conduct for all mankind, wherein the institution of polygamy is denounced or even spoken of with disapprobation.' "

Disciple : " But in this day and age of the world,

do you think it advisable for one to take upon his hands more than one wife ? Is this really the best solution of the marriage question?"

Evangelist: "I can answer that to your utmost satisfaction, and you will say I am right. You know, if you are posted in this matter, that more females reach the age of twenty than males. The former are not so much exposed — are not subjected to so many hazards. According to the Massachusetts reports, we find twenty-one per cent. more females than males. You understand that war and such causes sweep off the male population. Besides this, men do not marry as readily as women. Business, vice, love of freedom and other causes deter men from matrimony. So that many (I might, perhaps, say most) do not marry till from thirty to thirty-five, and very many not till thirty-eight or forty; while women are eligible at twenty, and most women are married at twenty-five, if at all. All in all, there are two females eligible to marriage to one male, and the only way the former can be properly cared for is by our system of plural marriage. Mormons do not often have more than two wives. Some have three or four, and even as high as seven and eight. Brigham Young really had but eighteen, though more than this has been attributed to him. The one that made him so much trouble was probably never duly confirmed. As a matter of fact, the husband, in many cases, is little more than a curator of those who are placed under his protection as wives. Our plural system of marriage is veritably a benign provision of our religion, since it cares for those who would otherwise be thrown upon the world defenseless and helpless."

Disciple: "Well, really, it's hard for women to be left to the world's doubtful mercy, and in this view it would seem that a man, to be 'square' with the female race, should be a Mormon. But I have read statistics that show, taking the country as a whole, both west and east, that the number of men about equals that of women; and I am told that here in Utah there are fully as many men as women, and that, of the two, the men are more anxious to get wives than the women are to get husbands. Now when several thousand polygamists get two or more wives and the priests and elders of the church get five or six (or perhaps ten or a dozen) of the most eligible of the females, really isn't it some of the men that are going to get left out in the cold?"

Seeing that my expounder of the faith looked puzzled, I continued:

"But is the paragon of domestic felicity attained by this practice? I should suppose a man's wife would recalcitrate, or 'kick,' as the boys say, when she sees another woman coming into the house."

Evangelist: "Well, I can tell you about that" [recovering his original self-possession]. "Formerly it was necessary to get the consent of the first wife, and all preceding, when a new one was taken; but now, on account of the persecutions to which Mormons are being subjected, the church sanctions marriages without the consent of previous wives. In many cases, indeed, the first or antecedent wives know nothing of the existence of others taken later. For example, I have now in mind a man in this city who has a wife here, one in Provo, and still another at another place, and not one of these knows of the existence of the others. The church now sanctions these concealed unions on account of its persecutions. A jealous wife, for instance, might make disclosures which would subject the innocent husband to the penalties of unrighteous laws."

Disciple: "Do you think the Edmunds law of 1882, and the still more stringent Edmunds-Tucker law of 1887, are materially affecting polygamy? From reports it would seem that these federal enactments had crowded Mormons rather hard."

Evangelist: "In one sense they have, perhaps, since, after the passage of these laws a large number of the most conscientious Mormons, including a good many high officers of the church, rather than be untrue to their convictions and to escape persecution, fled from the country, or at least retired from this city. There are, however, temporary set-backs to all true religious progress, but in our case these reverses are more apparent than real. You see, Gentiles are not in a position to know the actual state of things. As I said before, concealed marriages are now permitted, and really our cause is going right on, only less openly."

Seeing, on the part of my instructor a little show of reluctance to talk on these delicate topics, and fearing that I was prying too much into family affairs for the success of my experiment, I turned the subject by observing:

"Now, professor, when quite a young boy I remember of reading with great interest the original revelation of Joseph Smith, or a part of it at least, and I think it said somewhere that a man should have only one wife."

THE TEMPLE.

Evangelist: "Exactly! It says: 'There shall not any man among you have save it be one wife, and concubines he shall have none; for I, the Lord God, delighteth in the chastity of woman.' But understand this was all done away with by the later revelation, authorizing plural marriage."

Disciple: "I know; so I had heard. But when the later revelation came out, you know the people made a great fuss about it, and said they would not accept, as it contradicted the first revelation, and they thought it scandalous. When Brigham Young and Joseph Smith saw what an uproar the new doctrine was creating, you know they came out and publicly declared that no such new revelation had been received authorizing polygamy."

Evangelist: "I see your difficulty and will explain. When the second revelation was made, enjoining celestial marriage, it was seen by the president and his counselors that the people were not prepared for the new doctrine, and hence it seemed advisable to keep the new revelation concealed until the people could be educated to it."

Disciple: "But was it right for Brigham Young to tell the people that no such revelation had been received when it was found unpopular?"

Evangelist: "Most assuredly! Anything is right that enhances the glory of the Lord. We have this revelation: 'Under certain circumstances the Lord allows the priesthood to lie in order to save his people.' It is as when parents deceive their children when they seek to know things unsuited to their age, don't you see?"

Disciple: "Well, Mr. R——, you are posted to a letter on your religion. I certainly couldn't have hit upon any one better able to enlighten me. But, candidly, wouldn't it seem that the Lord ought not to have given the revelation until the people were ready

THE TABERNACLE.

for it? Then the priests and elders wouldn't have been placed under the necessity of telling any lies."

Evangelist: "But we can not question the motives of the Almighty, and it is not for us to pass judgment upon his methods. His ways are not our ways."

Disciple: "But I would like to inquire a little further, if I am not encroaching too much upon your time,"

Evangelist: "Certainly not. This is my business, and I am only too glad to have questions asked and see people interested in our religion. What had you specially in mind?"

Disciple: "At the time of the reformation in '55 and '56 you know it's a matter of history that young girls of a dozen years of age were enticed or forced to marry; that women were divorced and remarried almost daily, and that even the elders and others in high official rank exchanged wives, or what amounted to that—the divorce from one meaning marriage to another. Now the question is: Does the church of to-day approve of such things? I am told there is nothing in your code that even prevents a father from marrying his own daughter, and that a man often does marry a mother and her daughter or two sisters, and that there is one case here where a man actually married three generations—daughter, mother and grandmother. How about these things—are they considered proper now?"

Evangelist: "These things have been exaggerated; but so long as all marriages and divorces have to be confirmed by the church and thus receive the sanction of the Almighty, there can be no danger of going wrong in these matters. Our ideas of morality and right must not be set up against those of the Almighty. This is a common error. The Lord establishes the conditions of right and wrong. We have nothing to do with this."

Disciple: "Well! upon my word, professor, I

BEE HIVE HOUSE.

never saw a man clear up dark spots in the way you do. Do you think I would make a good Mormon?"

Evangelist: "Most assuredly, and if you wish to join——"

Disciple: "But one word, doctor, while I think of it. You know Joseph Smith received two revelations—the first prohibiting polygamy, the second permitting it. Now, was the first revelation a bogus one? Of course, one or the other of these revelations must have been a false one, since, when two things contradict each other, only one can be true. In one case it says it is *not* lawful to have more than one wife, in the other it says it *is* lawful ; so that it must be Smith was not inspired on one or the other of these occasions. How *is* that ?"

Evangelist : "Here is where our adversaries fall into a gross error. The original revelation was given by the Holy Spirit and was just as truly inspired as the second one, but when a new revelation is made contradicting a former one, the *new* supplants the old —a new dispensation is inaugurated and former things are no more."

Disciple: "Really, doctor, I am surprised at your facility in straightening out these difficulties ; but it does seem that the Almighty, who sees the end from the beginning, would have had the discretion not to spring a doctrine upon his people so prematurely, and thus stir up so much bad blood among them."

THE DEVELOPMENT OF THE GODS.

Evangelist : "Ah ! here is where you stumble by not understanding the mystery of creation and the nature of the Gods. We believe in the eternity of matter, the transmission of spirits, the evolution of spirit from refined matter, and in one sense a plurality of Gods. When you come to understand these mysteries you will not raise such questions. Further, we have a doctrine which might be termed 'The development of the Gods.' An understanding of this doctrine would especially clear up this difficulty."

Reflecting to myself that gods who do such things ought to be further developed, or rather, radically reformed, I continued the inquest — all the while

THE GREAT SALT LAKE

maintaining a spirit of entire satisfaction with his erudition—though constantly troubled by some new and unexplained difficulty.

Disciple: "But Mr. R——, here is a thing that greatly bothers me. Scripture says (and you tell me this is authority with you) that 'God can not lie.' Now if he is this infallible and righteous Being supposed, it would really seem that he could not be so thoughtless as to give his beloved priesthood a revelation that would necessitate their violating his commandments. It also says: 'There shall in no wise enter into it (the kingdom of heaven) anything that defileth, neither whatsoever worketh abomination or maketh a lie,' and 'All liars shall have their part in the lake' and so forth. Now, in all candor, professor, does it seem right to you that the Almighty should place his servants in a position where they were *forced* to lie, and then mete out terrible punishment to them hereafter for so doing?"

Evangelist: [With sudden emphasis] "But you see we are no judges of these mysteries. Probably all falsehoods told for his glory will be forgiven in the next world. You see we ought not to talk about things so far beyond us."

Disciple: "Well, doctor, I want to study this a little more. I am not quite clear. You understand I don't wish to be hasty and would like to give the subject more thought. Now as I have taken up a good deal of your time I wish to express my great gratitude for your pains and the instructive information you have imparted."

So saying, I took friendly leave of the voluble, but not over discreet, yet thoroughly indoctrinated Evangel, who, at the same time, handed forth a number of tracts that would enable me to become a Mormon on an approved plan.

Such are the sophistries and absurdities of Mormonism. A religious sect that reduces the supreme being to the low intellectual and moral level of a mendacious and dissolute human nature is certainly not too good to reduce woman to the basest slavery, or too patriotic to array itself in opposition to wholesome moral restraints and in defiance of just laws.

CHAPTER XIII.

STATEHOOD FOR UTAH.

In my effort to study the influence of the "Mormon idea" on the home, I have found everything so pledged to secrecy that nothing very demonstrative could be gathered from actual observation. Hence, nearly all the information gleaned in this direction has been from the testimony of others. For this reason I have no desire to detail the uncanny revelations of Mormon domestic life; but if half the stories of the agony and heartburn of Mormon wives and mothers be true, and there is much reason to believe the half has not been told, we can not wonder at the righteous indignation which prompted Miss Carmichael to say, 'If I were a man as I am a woman, I would stand in the halls of congress and cry aloud for the miserable women of Utah till the world should hear and know the wrongs and miseries of polygamy."

But one of the most significant specimens of "indoor" Mormonism is the recent clamor for statehood. This scheme was started over two years ago, and in spite of all the discouragements and set-backs which their cause has received, the Mormon leaders seem as noisy as ever for "equality of rights" among the states. The average Mormon is especially insistant about having his "rights," but none have yet been discovered who were willing to receive their just de-

EAGLE GATE.

serts. Their "rights" being generally defined by revelation from on high, are dangerous to trifle with.

Some features of this movement for getting into the union are most remarkable and worthy of study.

Since the passage of the Edmunds law Mormons have found themselves too closely crowded for comfort and have become extremely apprehensive for the safety of their cherished creed. In this dilemma a new idea struck the Mormon camp like one of Jove's fresh-forged thunderbolts. It seemed to occur to the whole body politic of Mormondom, all at once, at a bound and without warning, that the territory must be converted into a state and this without delay. It was whispered around among the "saints": "We will be better off as a state than under the present territorial laws that so interfere with our 'rights.' We can then elect our own governor and dictate more or less as to our judges and juries and control nearly all the offices of power ; and then these accursed Gentiles can't make us so much trouble. Yes, statehood ! that's the thing—that will help us out—that's the best thing devised yet and we'll have it or die."

So, without discussing the matter through the press or in any way advising with the non-Mormon element, they organized a "People's party," and, like the traditional spider, invited the Democrats and Republicans of the Gentile persuasion to join them in their efforts to secure statehood for Utah. But the motives of the scheme were too patent and their proposal was as promptly rejected as it had been suddenly conceived. The Gentile committees of both parties also had the courage to offer in their replies to the bold proposition of their presumptuous opponents a few well-directed suggestions and as many more instructive reflections on their course and conduct. But an "all-wool" Mormon is

AMELIA PALACE

never silenced when his "rights" are at stake. Notwithstanding the poor consolation which the cause thus received at home and the scant encouragement it has since had from the federal government, these religio-political operators still persist, fully convinced that statehood is the only feasible way out of their dilemma.

The constitution which they drafted to be operative

in the new state is, like their creed, full of puzzles and perplexities. The article on polygamy is especially deserving of the attention of political economists. At one fell stroke of a pen ("divinely guided," I suppose) this solemn declaration is put on record:

"Bigamy and polygamy being considered incompatible with a republican form of government, each of them is hereby forbidden and declared a misdemeanor."

What could be more unexpected and confounding than this? That Mormons, who have been so unyielding in this matter for forty years, should come out with such a declaration! Astonishing! Does this really mean the dawn of reformation in Utah? But before we become entirely lost in bewilderment, let us examine a little and be assured that the Mormon sage has not worked in his usual trap-door attachment.

"Bigamy and polygamy!" what do they mean? It just occurs that when the writer used these terms when interviewing the priesthood, they were almost invariably repeated by the latter in such expressions as "plural marriage" or "celestial marriage." The evangelist even took the pains to politely explain that they did not call the taking of more than one wife polygamy, but plural marriage. The Mormon notion of polygamy is the marriage of two or more wives without the sanction of the church; but when confirmed by the priest (and hence by heaven) the marriage to more than one woman is simply "plural" or "celestial"—or as sometimes termed "patriarchal." So when they make declarations against bigamy and polygamy they evidently mean that they are in favor of punishing "outsiders" who have more than one wife. I don't find anything in their constitution about punishing the act of "plural" or "celestial" marriage

LION'S HEAD ROCK, GREAT SALT LAKE.

Even bigamy and polygamy, as they use the terms, are seemingly less grave offenses than commonly supposed, since they reduce them from crimes or felonies (as treated in all the states) to misdemeanors. Hence even these, while punishable as misdemeanors, would not debar their perpetrators from the right to vote and hold office—thus nullifying the Edmunds act. This, to all appearances, is one of their trap-door arrangements. There are, however, those who claim that it is not in order to pass judgment on the intentions of the committee in reference to bigamy and polygamy. In the absence of actual knowledge, say they, these terms must be construed in the usual sense.

But how much does this better the situation? Assume that these terms in the ambiguous document refer to "plural marriage." We then have the charming attitude of a people declaring against one of the fundamental doctrines of their creed and pronouncing it a misdemeanor at the same time that they hold it as a divine revelation, teach it from their pulpits, practice it in defiance of law and vehemently denounce the government for interfering with their belief. Surely "he who laughs last laughs best," when analyzing a Mormon's declaration of principles. In this charitable view of Mormon intentions, their church articles and convention resolutions furnish most intoxicating pabulum for thought. For example, one of their public documents says:

"Among the principles of our religion is that of immediate revelation from God; one of the doctrines so revealed is celestial or plural marriage, for which ostensibly we are stigmatized and hated. This is a *vital* part of our religion, the decision of the courts notwithstanding."

Again, in a late address of the church, it is de-

STATEHOOD FOR UTAH. 211

TRAMWAY IN LITTLE COTTONWOOD CAÑON.

clared: "We can not, at the behest of men, lay aside those great principles which God has communicated to us, nor violate those sacred and eternal covenants which we have entered into for time and eternity." The chief and essential one of these "great principles" and "eternal covenants," which all full-stock Mormons have "entered into for time and eternity," is polygamy or "celestial" marriage, which is declared to be a "*vital* part" of their religion. This "*vital* part" of their religion they now pronounce a misdemeanor. Was there ever such an anomaly? This surely can not be the intent of the committee, for a full-fledged Mormon would hardly be expected to proclaim his favorite dogma a misdemeanor. Still public sentiment is divided on this point, and there seems to be no way to settle the question except by giving the Mormons statehood, when the solons of Utah will be ready and willing to interpret their mysterous oracles.

But one other circumstance favoring the explanation first given is, that no one half-tutored in Mormon conjury ever suspects a "saint" politician of using English in its usual or accepted sense when referring to polygamy, or anything else in which he attempts to pledge himself or party to fair dealing or correct living.

Another peculiar feature of this strange document is its painful silence on the subject of "unlawful cohabitation." Nearly all the arrests and convictions thus far made have been for this offense, on account of the difficulties in the way of proving the crime of polygamy — all marriages being performed in the church without witnesses and by priests pledged to secrecy. Strange that earnest Mormons, anxious for the suppression of these unhallowed practices, should have omitted to provide penalties for, or even pronounce against, this offense—especially since it has proved almost the only avenue through which successful prosecution has been made. It is hard to escape the conviction that this omission is also one of their "trap-doors."

In another place in their constitution these astute diplomats have inserted a provision that the grade of the offense—polygamy—shall not be raised above that in the instrument, namely, a misdemeanor. This protects the derelict Mormon for all time, so that he may vote and hold office, whatever betides him in his vicious career. It is hard to understand how patriots of the "People's party," posing as anti-polygamists, should go so far out of their way to secure such a signal advantage for their opponents. It must be this is another of their trap-doors.

The committee who framed this new constitution for Utah is alleged to be made up of *monogamous* Mormons, and for this reason it is thought by some that honesty of purpose characterizes their fair professions. But it should be borne in mind that there is not so much difference at heart between a monogamist Mormon and one of plural or "celestial" propensities. All polygamists were once monogamists, and the monogamist of to-day may decide to take to himself an extra help-meet to-morrow. It is well known here that the monogamists, as a class, uphold and connive at the doings of the polygamists; are working in their interest and in the cherished hope of restoring their leaders from exile, and seeing them returned to power. The Mormon hierarchy would be in sorry plight indeed without this grimalkin's paw. But all the plausibility which the scheme possesses from its being pushed by this element of the church, vanishes when it is understood that the latter maintains the same belief in regard to those "sacred and eternal covenants" held by their polygamous brethren; that they affiliate with them; champion their cause on the sly, and in various ways labor to carry out their behests and strengthen the power of the church by secretly nurturing the "essential part" of its creed. Added to this is the suspicion which must necessarily attach to the intents and motives of a body of representative (?) men who would indite so incoherent and ambiguous a document as the "new constitution." No one here versed in Mormon legerdemain is at all misled or in the least puzzled to decipher the purpose and purport of their fair-faced declarations.

But it is asked: To what extent is polygamy now practiced in Utah? This is a difficult question to answer definitely, since opinion is so divided. If we accept the version of the Mormon evangelist, who so freely discussed the religion and practice of the church, of which I gave an account in the last chapter, it would appear that the Edmunds law is doing little more than to induce privacy in the unlawful practice. Still there was the plain inference that their cause had received a set-back, which in his view was only one of those temporary reverses incident to true religious progress. There can be no rational doubt that polygamy is practiced clandestinely and to a wide extent. The Edmunds law has nevertheless accomplished much — indeed, has so demoralized the file and rank of the Mormon cohorts that their captains and commanders are badly prostrated. Their commander-in-

WEBER CAÑON

chief found it so hot for him at the capital that he fled from the country, and many of his followers followed suit. Under this salutary law nearly six hundred indictments were made from the time of its passage in 1882 to 1887, inclusive, all but about five per cent of which were for unlawful cohabitation — the five per cent being for polygamy. About half of these indictments resulted in conviction. Among those who have taken the oath to abide by the law, it is believed that a great part have lived up to their pledges. Others who would not take the oath at all, and who have been convicted and imprisoned for these unlawful practices, have even refused all offers of immunity from punishment on condition of future obedience to the law. These are the "holy martyrs," or, as some call them, "holy tearers."

Of all the pitiable sights in this country the most heart-rending is that of a Mormon martyr. He seems to be a sort of nondescript genus, belonging to a class of men who are "a law unto themselves." Denied the object of his lust, he walks right up to the prison door and takes his place in the dark and narrow cell, stiff-necked and stiff-backed, refusing to compromise his conscience and manhood by agreeing to be a law-abiding citizen. What a heroic example of fidelity to principle and fealty to personal conviction! Poor martyr to conscience! Persecuted in an enlightened age for refusing to give up his libidinous career and live a life of respectability and honor! If it wasn't for his conscience the government and he could deal and come to amicable terms. But conscience forbids the martyr

ECHO CAÑON.

to abandon one of the most degrading practices in the category of crimes and commands him to dethrone woman from her high estate, debase motherhood and heap Pandora's box high with mischief to the rising generation. This is what puzzles the wiseacres. There is a general prejudice in this country against interfering with a man's religion, or punishing him for conscience sake. This is where the Mormon martyr has all the way been at an advantage. If he had simply complained of being abused for being caught at his neighbor's hen-roost or for toting off his neighbor's sheep at midnight, the case could have been disposed of at once. But instead, it has been the case of a man whose conscience forbade him to forsake the "hot-bed of corruption" in which he wallowed and substitute therefor a clean and manly life. If he had simply taken the ground that he was terribly misused and maltreated for practicing the less flagrant offences of incendiarism or cruelty to animals; or had he even posed as a picture of persecution because the government wouldn't allow him to commit rapine and murder, there would have been little of all this trouble and perplexity. But when a man sets up the plea of conscience, even though it be for the devastation of human hearts and the wreck of human souls, we hear the cry: "Hands off." But it seems that the government is becoming of late more and more disposed to deal summarily with these bad cases of conscience, and this is what spreads such consternation throughout the Mormon ranks.

 Among the fruits of my effort to study Mormon

A ROMANTIC RETREAT, AMERICAN FORK CAÑON.

character — especially that of the polygamists, I find, first, that they must be credited with consistency. They are consistent in two things — in being "first, last and all the time" in favor of having all the wives they want, and in wanting the government to let them have their own way about it. Second, I find a trace of sincerity — they sincerely desire to be allowed free course in gratifying their depraved lusts and low ambitions. Third, they are not hypocrites — so far as concerns their favorite doctrine. They believe in this abomination, and instead of practicing one thing and preaching another, they come boldly forward and proclaim to the world that these abominations are "an essential part of their creed," and that they have entered into them "for time and eternity." No hypocrisy about that! The average monogamist Mormon, perhaps, shares these same sentiments, but he lacks the sincerity and frankness to openly avow it. Should he later decide to enter the blissful state of celestial matrimony, he will not be likely to revise his professions in the midst of present complications. So, really, the three redeeming traits mentioned belong distinctively to the polygamist.

But what kind of people are these Mormons anyway? is the question so often asked. In general it may be answered: About ninety per cent are foreigners. Thus far the writer has come in contact with few Americans among them. Many foreigners come to this territory to avail themselves of the flattering promises of Mormonism and in the hope of bettering their condition. About one-half of the sect is made up of the subservient vassals of the church. These are in the main ignorant, superstitious and easily imposed upon, everything coming from the priesthood being to them law and gospel. They are, as a rule, under complete subjection to the hierarchy and go and come at their nod and beck. Then there is the more intelligent and "nothing-to-lose" class, who have failed in business or religion, or both, or perhaps in some other way become objects of suspicion in church and society, and hence are ready for adventure. These might perhaps be fitly designated as the "dead-beat" brigade. They are far less profitable than the vassals, being less useful and less reliable. Next above these comes the army of Mormon officers, such as the "first presidents," "bishops," "high-priests," "seventies," "patriarchs," "apostles," and the like — constituting, all told, nearly one-third of the adult population. They are the leaders and men of influence. Some of them are fanatics — the evangelist that I interviewed, for example — some, bigots, and some — well — yes — if you will have it — rascals. "Bad men will get into the church." These men put on long faces, and wish to have it understood that they are en rapport with heaven. The fact is, their infamous and absurd doctrines come from the other direction. They complain of being persecuted and pose as martyrs to conscience. As a matter of fact, they are simply martyrs to lust — lust for power and lust for woman. The spectacle of such men setting up the plea of conscience is as pathetic as that of a wild African boar poring over the leaves of a prayer-book; or that of a bland Florida crocodile posting up on the Westminster catechism. It's difficult to say which is most deserving of our sympathy. God speed the day when the last vestige of this national disgrace shall be wiped out.

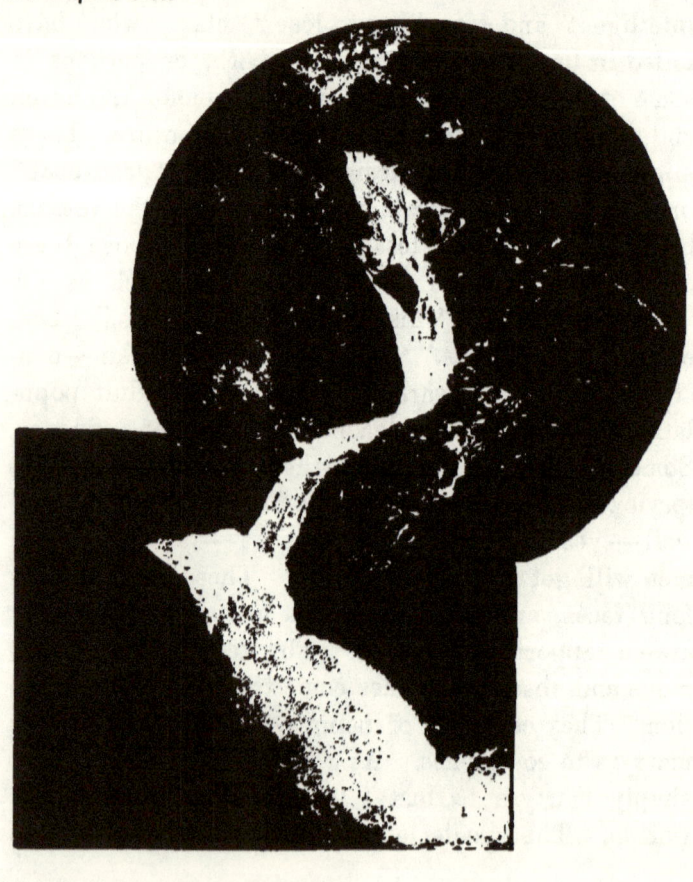

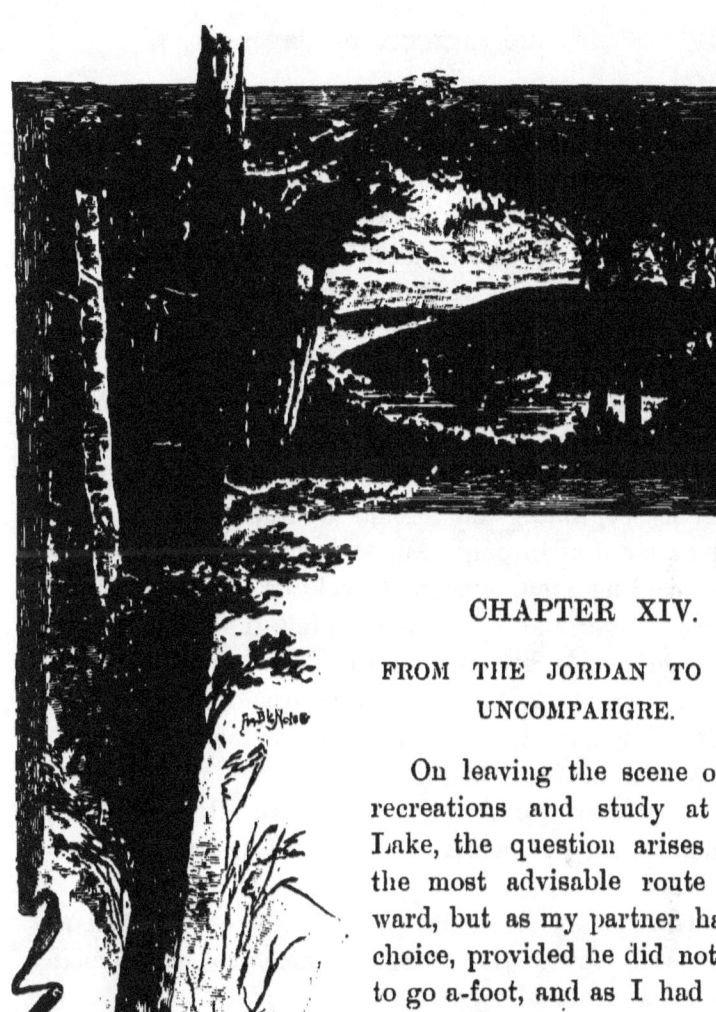

CHAPTER XIV.

FROM THE JORDAN TO THE UNCOMPAHGRE.

On leaving the scene of our recreations and study at Salt Lake, the question arises as to the most advisable route eastward, but as my partner had no choice, provided he did not have to go a-foot, and as I had none, providing we took the Denver & Rio Grande, the matter was quickly and peaceably settled. The forenoon ride was through a rich agricultural region along the valley of the Jordan. The Mormons are as industrious as they are forbearing, and the fruits of their persevering toil is seen in rich farm lands made productive by their unremitting efforts. Our journey in this cheerful region lay between the Wasatch range at the eastward, and the Oquirrh Mountains at the west, while in the vicinity of Provo, lofty Nebo suggestively rises above his neighbors in an attitude of true sublimity.

Having taken dinner at Provo, the eating station, near Utah Lake, we are soon brought to Spanish Fork Cañon, the point of departure from the Utah Valley, whence, beginning the ascent up the Spanish Fork River, we pass through a picturesque cañon, bordered by receding mountains and rocky walls. The train moves slower and slower as we climb the steeps, but a forty-mile ride brings us in due time to Soldier Summit at an elevation of seven thousand five hundred feet. Descending from the height, we soon find ourselves in the remarkable cañon of the Price River. This we follow for fifty miles, and to within a short distance of its mouth, where it empties into the Green.

The scenery along the river is not only peculiar, but really bewildering. One becomes so accustomed to certain natural forms that when approaching a new mountain or river scene, he expects a recurrence of certain configurations with which his senses have become familiarized; but now he is suddenly confronted by contours and colors for which he had never stipulated in his anticipation, and is therefore utterly confounded by the strange combinations, of novelty,

CASTLE GATE.

beauty and sublimity which are here presented. The Price River madly dashes and foams among the rocks at his side, and the walls of the cañon rise more abrupt and menacing as the descent continues. The cañon, too, grows deeper, the train crosses and recrosses the winding stream, there is a premonition that something is coming, and the traveler is kept in constant suspense. Nearly every passenger throws aside his object of diversion within to see what is brewing without. Windows are thrown up, heads projected and platforms crowded. What means the commotion? Presently the mystery is resolved, and we behold in front of us the majestic pillars of Castle Gate, commanding the entrance to Castle Cañon. Two massive walls of red-stained granite rear themselves to a height on one side of four hundred and fifty and on the other five hundred feet — walls that might be supposed to have been built by human art, but of such magnificent proportions that one can not but feel that human enterprise would be unequal to the task. But wonderful as it is, and regarded, as it often is, the climax of the scenes along the cañon of the Price River, it appealed to the writer's sense as a felicitous introduction to still greater marvels beyond.

The phenomena which greet the tourist in Castle Cañon are so unique, unexpected and unheard-of that he can only gaze and exclaim: "unaccountable!" Here he sees what may be easily likened to the Roman Coliseum, or the ruins of Luxor and Baalbec. Carried back to feudal times, we have unmistakably the strong-holds of the feudal lords with their moats and battlements, their heights and magnitudes, which Scott in his stately language so delights to describe. Here indeed are kingdoms and commonwealths honeycombed with royal edifices. As we ride for two hours through these mystic confines, we discover in the course of the journey, walls and parapets beyond which the imagination converts the grotesque forms of rock into projecting tops of castles, cathedrals, temples and Babel towers. To the right, before reaching Green River station, in the distance, are, to all appearances, perpen-

UNCOMPAHGRE RIVER.

dicular walls, immense squares and blocks of hewn stone — manifold configurations that are easily converted into military fortifications, church spires and domes — in fact, almost any species of architecture the mind would recall, from Gothic to Egyptian, from Queen Anne to Yahoo.

Castle Cañon is a veritable wonderland, unique in

that its mountain-height, rocky formations approach so closely in form to the architectural designs of man. These are not entirely of a fantastic order, for we find outlines of seeming geometrical accuracy. There are vast mesas of rock, resembling blocks of buildings in the form of oblong squares or circles, rising perpendicularly from massive abutments, several hundred feet in height and with tops apparently as level as a billiard table. Then we see avenues of buildings laid out like so many gigantic adobe dwellings, forming a Mexican municipality on an extraordinary scale, with plazas and palaces added.

Sluggish, indeed, is the imagination that can view this strange phenomena without drawing from the remarkable formations a host of similitudes of human handicraft. In other parts of the country we find similar rock formations, but nowhere, extending over so great a terrritory, are there such striking architectural designs, such rock-hewn cities, such stupendous magnitudes, such unrivaled sublimity.

As the sun sets over the western peaks a scene of indescribable beauty transfigures the castellated walls and towers that stand so bold and black against the clear-cut sky. My traveling companion now gets into one of his enthusiastic moods, and earnestly maintains that the castle of Torquilston has either been resurrected from the dusky past and reinstated here on the western desert, or else Scott had this in mind from the beginning. For he declares that he can catch through the gloaming a glimpse of the Jewess Rebecca, standing on the high parapet in stately mien, welcoming the dizzy depth below as an escape from the brutal templar, Bois Guilbert. As the sun sinks closer to the mountain-top, its reflecting beams set this same castle ablaze, and now we have the transcendent

ON THE RESERVATION.

scene of a vast conflagration far in the distant horizon. The Secretary protests that he now sees the maniacal Ulrici, just as Scott describes her, in the guise of one of the furies, with long, disheveled hair flowing from her naked head, her arms tossing in wild exultation as if she reigned empress of the conflagration she had raised. I objected to all this as overdrawn; but he would not yield an iota, asseverating that it was all there. Former experiences had taught me the indiscretion of interfering with his mental recreations, and as I had myself found in these rock-formed prodigies so many suggestions of the strange and incredible, it was poorly in place to attempt to dispossess my comrade of these delusions, if such they were.

The west-bound tourist over the Denver & Rio Grande is signally favored in the time-card arrangements, which admits of seeing the greatest objects of interest throughout the length of the main line by day. Just as we had passed the land of castle wonders, darkness, heavy eyelids, and somewhat overwrought imaginations, all advised retirement and rest, which came most refreshingly.

At about three o'clock the following morning, we were waked according to orders to disembark at Montrose — the only stop-off that we made from Salt Lake to Colorado Springs. The motives inspiring the self-sacrifice implied in the mention of this early hour were none other than those of personal friendship. A man must indeed have a strong hold on the writer's affection to make possible such an infraction of his long fossilized practices. After restlessly wearing out the balance of the night and breakfasting at the hotel, we were met by our old friend, F. D. Catlin, Esq., the County Judge, and one of the progressive young men of the west. Hospitality runs riot in Colorado, and the delightful way these days at Montrose were variously occupied, in grateful rest at the elegant residence of our friend, driving about on the plains and among the mountains, overhauling the past and making the living present interesting to the fleet coyote and the bounding roebuck, is simply *mirabile dictu*.

Montrose is a most promising town of one thousand five hundred inhabitants, situated in the fertile Uncompahgre Valley, once the favorite hunting ground of the Utes. The town is romantically situated in sight of the Rockies, whose snowy summits gleam in the morning sun, far to the east. At the south are the San Juan Mountains, towering heaven-high and guarded by the two Titan sentinels, Sneffles and Uncompahgre, both of which are over fourteen thousand feet above the sea. On the west are the Uncompahgre plateaus and peaks that extend far into limitless space, until broken by the cañon of the Grand River, one hundred and fifty miles away. Everything in nature about Montrose is wild and weird, and the tourist who would obtain one of the best pictures of contrast with eastern towns will find a brief stop-off in the Uncompahgre Valley a pleasant incident of his transcontinental tour.

CHAPTER XV.

OVER THE ROCKIES—MONTROSE TO MANITOU.

Taking leave of the Judge and his entertaining family who had made our visit to Montrose an occasion of uninterrupted pleasure, we again repaired to the iron track that is sure transport to

>"The mountains' everlasting wall
>Where the thunders waters fall,"

to
>"Beauties that elude the grasp,"

to
>"Gleams and glorious seen and lost."

The morning ride, however, was one of modest pretention. There were no overpowering flights of nature and hence nothing imperative to report, unless it be the mental uneasiness of an old lady in the seat just in front of us, who, whenever the train was about to pull out from the station, was constantly worried for fear the conductor might get left behind. From Montrose the road winds for some distance along the Uncompahgre Valley. The first station of importance is Cimarron, at the junction of the Cimarron Creek and Gunnison River, a noted hunting and trout region, the breakfast station and the point at which the open observation car is attached to the train. To the latter we repaired after repairing the wasted tissue incident to the long before-breakfast ride. Such a deserving meal as is set before the traveler at Cimarron should not be passed by unnoticed. Wild game and trout and excellent cuisine generally, constituted the bill of fare. The tourist who so far forgets himself as to take it for granted that he is in a cowless region of the remote west and calls for sky blue milk without minnows, is surprised to find his order responded to by a glowing goblet of creamy nectar, containing neither a trace of struggling life nor a "reflection of heaven's own blue." Everything else is of the same order, and in fact all the eating stations on the line reflect credit upon their management.

The Black Cañon extends from Cimarron to Sapinero, at the latter place the observation car being detached. The elements constituting the distinctive features of this cañon are the perpendicularity of its walls, their extraordinary height, which in places is from two to three thousand feet, and the no less extraordinary length through which the remarkable phenomenon prevails, being nearly twenty miles in extent. Added to these are the beautifully polished pink-painted surfaces of rock, and the peculiar configurations of the lines of separation, which, are variously smooth, straight, contorted, twisted and tied in knots. There is also the wild scene in the bed of the deep sea-green river, where its foam-crested waters surge and rave, leaping into the air, dashing against the vermillion walls and tearing about with reckless indifference to everything in its way.

Among the landmarks of the Black Cañon are Chippeta Falls, that leap over the rocky walls of the cañon, the sport of winds, much after the manner of the Yose-

APPROACH TO THE BLACK CAÑON.

mite Cascades, and Currecanti Needle. The latter is a conical tower somewhat in relief from the walls of the river and appearing to the observer like a massive obelisk rising out of the depths. Its lower proportions are such that its true loftiness is obscured by the massiveness of the base. It is, however, none the less deserving of minute attention and if time admitted, of careful study. It is of pink-red color and the substance of the rock forming it, like the walls of the cañon, are of extreme hardness.

Some distance beyond the Black Cañon is the delightfully situated town of Gunnison, commanding scenery of marked beauty in the Rockies. From this point a few hours ride along the beautiful valley of the Tomichi River brings us to the steep grade that leads up to the back-bone of the country—the summit of the Rocky mountains, variously denominated the "dome," "crest" and vertebral column" of the continent. Here is the Great Divide and the melting snows close by diverge, one portion making its way towards the Pacific, the other seeking the far Atlantic. As we ascend in tortuous curves, peak rises above peak in front of us until, at the summit, called Marshall Pass, nearly 11,000 feet above the sea we catch, on emerging from the snow sheds, a passing conception of what constitutes the upper Rockies — numberless peaks, countless domes, an infinity of undulating waves, fixed as the foundations of the earth in which they are set. At certain points on the western slope four distinct lines of the railroads are plainly seen. Some idea of the difficulties encountered in overcoming this highest

IN THE BLACK CAÑON.

barrier of the Rockies may be conceived from the fact that in places we ride a mile or more to gain a dozen rods, the steepest part of the ascent having a grade of 220 feet. Descending on the opposite side towards the valley of the Arkansas, grand vistas of mountain scenery open up before the expectant observer. Dark-visaged Ouray rises bold and aggressive to the north while the snowy peaks of the Sangre de Christo undulate along the southern sky until lost in the far horizon.

At Salida, the junction of the "Leadville Branch," a passenger from the far-famed mining town boards the train and reports the strange providence which, but the day before had swept a citizen of Leadville into eternity by the bursting of a boiler, and that too, while the victim was indulging in profanity. But it was argued that this was no providential occurrence whatever, since a bursting boiler could never get in its work on a Leadville man between his oaths.

But what next? As the clown said, "Something else," and it *is* something else, and something else remarkable all the way. Now, as we fly along the road-bed beyond Poncha and Salida, noted health and pleasure resorts cheerfully nestled among the mountains, we are hurried down into the Grand Cañon of the Arkansas. Here the Collegiate Range of mountains falls into the panoramic line of passing scenes—their highest peaks, Harvard, Princeton and Yale, lifting their whitened helmets over 14,000 feet in air. The scenery all along the cañon is marked with striking features, but the climax is only reached with the Royal

CURRECANTI NEEDLE.

Gorge. The whole cañon is a melodramatic sermon, seven miles long; but so well-conceived and such a masterpiece of eloquence that the audience is held in close attention to the last. The emerald waters of the Arkansas foam and rave in the terrible depths—the rubicund walls rise bold and threatening into the appalling heights. As the train advances the observer is more interested and more spell-bound, until breaking suddenly upon his rapt senses, the awe-inspiring chasm springs into full view. Emotion reigns with high hand and holds its reckless carnival in defiance of all efforts at self-control. Here we plunge down into a deep dark chasm, hemmed in by crimson walls of granite—down, down into the bowels of the earth,

> "Where Tartarus with sheer descent,
> Dips 'neath the ghost-world twice as deep
> As towers above Earth's continent,
> The heights of heaven's Olympian steep."

> "In front a portal stands displayed,
> On adamantine columns stayed;
> Nor mortal, nor immortal foe,
> These massy gates can overthrow."

Forward and downward we shoot, one thousand, now two, yes, almost three thousand feet below the top of the fissure, until Erebus seems close at hand, until reason is dethroned by delusion, sense by hallucination, and we almost involuntarily make the effort to be reconciled to the situation, and lay plans for a prospective tour through the infernal realms.

My traveling companion observes that if this really is the entrance to Tartarus, "How about the old fel-

MARSHALL PASS.

lows Theseus and Salmoneus, respectively, the restless adventurer and the hustling counterfeiter of Jove's thunder, who are said to be having a hard time of it in the nether world? Do you suppose we'll see 'em?"

This was one of the Secretary's overcharges of enthusiasm in which he always contemplates somewhat more than he can show for in the scene itself. As a matter of fact, however, the opposite picture—some of the scenes in the pleasure department of that lower world so pleasingly set forth by the Prince of Latin poets, is fairly well reproduced in the region entered through the Royal Gorge. The happily situated and scenery-invested Cañon City is now reached, and soon Pueblo, whence a short ride brings us to Colorado Springs, Pike's Peak, Manitou and the Garden of the Gods— or if you please Virgil's Elysian Fields. We may adopt Dryden's version with a little alteration and scarcely go amiss in our application; for here we merge from the chasm, where,

"Wide is the fronting gate and raised on high,
With adamantine columns, threats the sky."

From this auspicious exit our iron horse makes its way,

"Where long extended plains of pleasure lie,
Where verdant fields with those of heaven vie,
With ether vested and a purple sky ;
Where airy limbs in sport may exercise,
And on the green, contend the wrestler's prize.
Some in heroic verse divinely sing,
Others in artful measures lead the ring.
Here patriots live, who, for their country's good,
In fighting fields were prodigal of blood.
Here blameless men are wont to seek abode
And poets worthy their aspiring God."

ROYAL GORGE.

Like the realms described, the population of these delightful retreats is cosmopolitan, and the graces and amenities of the cultured portions of the world are honorably represented, from the scholar who can converse in seven languages to the wit who can hold his tongue in seventeen.

Among the interesting places near Manitou and Pike's Peak are "Glen Eyrie," "Seven Falls," "Cheyenne Mountain," "Seven Lakes," "Crystal Park," "Ruxton's Glen," "Red Rock Cañon," "Manitou Grand Caverns," "William's Cañon," "Cave of the Winds," "Rainbow Falls," "Ute Pass," "Cascade Cañon," "Green Mountain Falls," and "Manitou Park." North and South Cheyenne Cañons are about ten miles south of Manitou and possess rare attractions in the way of mountain scenery. In South Cheyenne Cañon are the "Seven Falls," and, near by, the Cheyenne toll road that leads to the "Seven Lakes." A short distance from the "Seven Falls," sequestered in one of nature's favorite sanctuaries, is the grave of the illustrious author of Ramona.

Cascade Cañon, Green Mountain Falls and Manitou Park are now reached from either Colorado

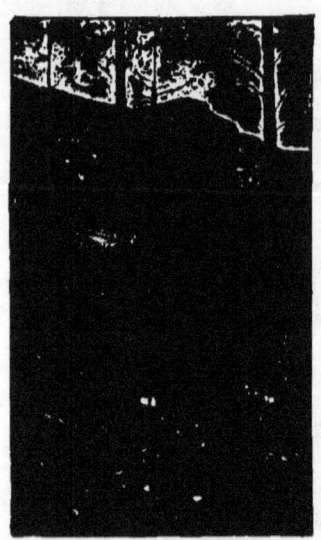

A REFRESHING SPRING, CASCADE CAÑON.

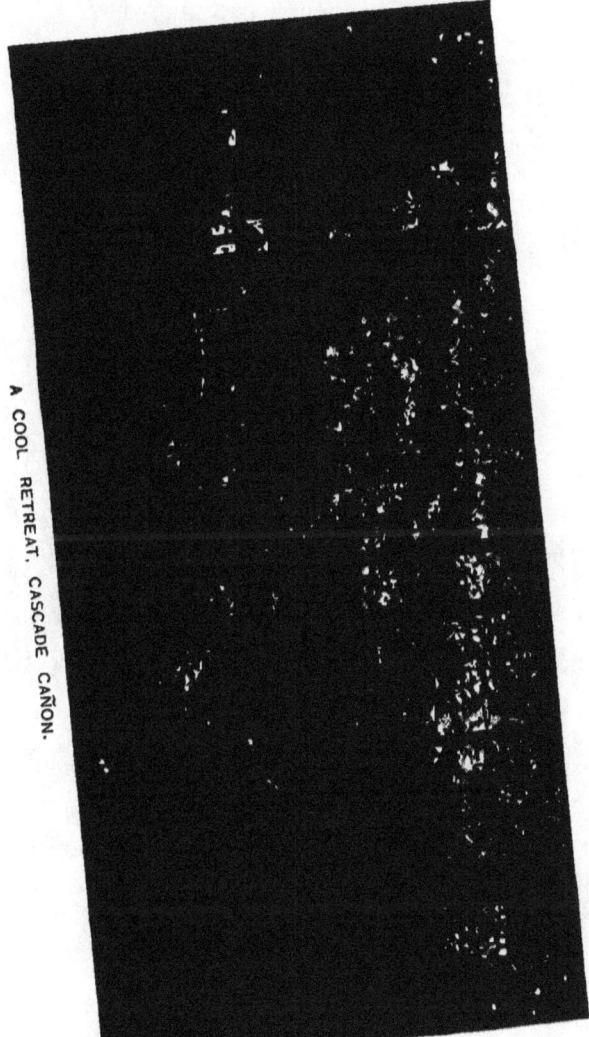

A COOL RETREAT, CASCADE CAÑON.

Springs or Manitou by the Colorado Midland Railway, which traverses the Ute Pass, amid wild scenery, and brings within easy access a number of noted places of interest. Stage connections are made at Green Mountain Falls Station with Manitou Park, a distance of

OVER THE ROCKIES. 247

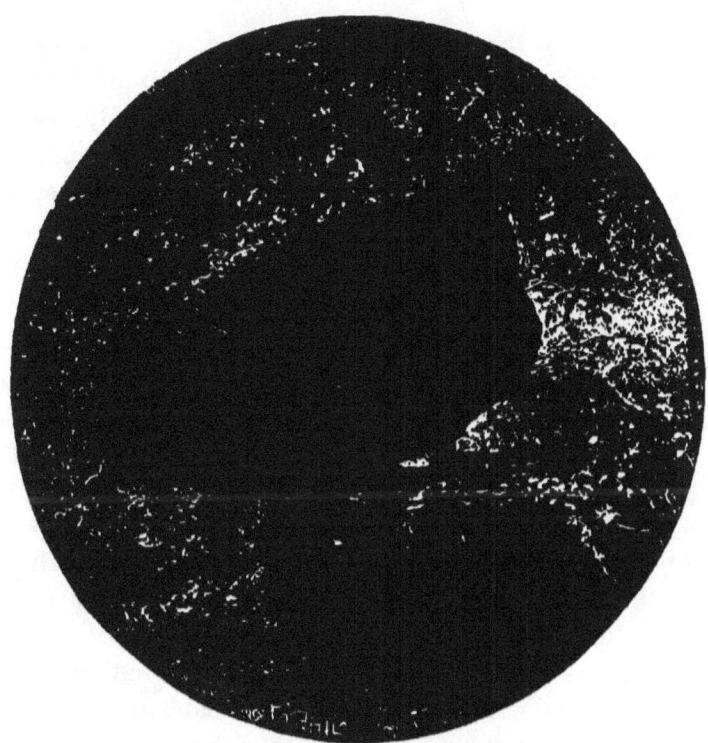

THE BALANCED ROCK.

seven miles. These cheerful summer resorts, invested with so much that is romantic and pleasing, have of late been growing in public favor, and are now much frequented by visitors from abroad. From Cascade Cañon a fine carriage road has been built to the summit of Pike's Peak, making the ascent of this monarch of the mountains a mere pastime. At the Halfway House and on the summit, refreshments are served to both man and beast. A short distance above the Half-way House is the "Balanced Rock," weighing tons, and the Devil's Leap," a noted precipice half a mile high. A few miles further on at Grand View, under a favoring atmosphere, may be seen Marshall Pass, ninety miles distant, and the black columns of smoke rising from the laboring engines as they pull over the grade. The outlook from Grand View and the summit (when the latter is not obscured by clouds) includes one of the finest panoramas of the West, presenting scenes of unsurpassed grandeur, to be enjoyed by the spectator, but beyond the pale of description.

The Grand Caverns are also reached by a carriage road extending to near the summit of one of the lesser peaks in the immediate vicinity of Manitou, being but a mile or two from the town and near the Ute Pass. About the same distance up Williams Cañon is another of these marvelous caverns where stalactite and stalagmite formations, glistening like polished horn, array themselves into the form of animals, fruits and flowers, and various works of art. The resemblance in some cases is so striking that the tourist almost suspects that human art is being passed as nature's caprice. Closer inspection, however, of these wonderful floral and other artistic designs, into which nature has so cleverly woven her matchless frost-work, reveals a beauty so consummate and a workmanship so masterly that doubt can no longer be entertained as to their origin.

Among the wonders in the vicinity of Manitou, the 'Garden of the Gods' is generally conceded a place at the head. But some find far more of interest in the strange phenomena than others. There is so much that is complex, varied and diversified that the average

MANITOU AND PIKE'S PEAK.

visitor is greatly perplexed. When it is considered that over an area of five hundred acres, and projecting to nearly all heights up to four hundred feet, rise an indefinite number of rose-colored mounds, monuments and gigantic monoliths, assuming almost every conceivable attitude, and presenting grotesque figures never conceived by the caricaturist, it must be admitted that we have encountered a veritable freak of nature. There are at least the elements of novelty and mystery, and if we stand within the crimson portals of the famous gates and view the snow-crowned Titan of the Rockies, or direct the gaze to any quarter of the horizon, we must also add the higher element of sublimity.

But it is not within the province of the writer's aim or the possibilities of his pen to fitly describe these romantic, scenery-intoxicating realms of myths and mysteries. To say that Colorado Springs is one of the most attractive towns in the region of the Rockies, to dwell upon the wholesome breadth of its thoroughfares and the luxuriant shade in which they are embowered—to enlarge upon its scenic attractions—to set forth the glory that clusters about mystic Manitou, the Garden of the Gods and their wild environments—all this would be little to the purpose. These places must be seen to be duly estimated and truly appreciated. So too with the wonderful caverns where nature seems to have made the effort, in some sportive mood, to mimic both human and barbaric art and where sweet music responds to the faint touch of her calcium harpsichord. Equally unsatisfactory is the vain attempt to detail the virtues of healing springs, the fascination of cañons and pleasure-paradises and the strange historical associations that make them enchanted ground. The weak media of human

ROCK FORMATIONS, GARDEN OF THE GODS.

thought can not grasp the changing forms, the Protean guises, the lights and shadows, the contrasts and complements—the strange blending of colors. It matters not with what fidelity the picture is drawn; all said and done and the grand galaxy of Nature's train of kaleidoscopic melodramas, remains a conception unconveyed—an enigma and a mystery still.

The journey from Salt Lake to Manitou—from the valley of the Jordan to the valley of the Arkansas—from Mount Nebo to Pike's Peak—is one unprecedented in the amount and variety of novel, unique and wonderful natural phenomena. We call it natural, because it is of nature, but much of it is so removed from preconceived conceptions that it might be fittingly termed unnatural. The tourist is constantly in a state of surprise and mingled astonishment, at times distrusting his own senses. The idea of seeing a vast amphitheatre, an imposing citadel or a colossal relic of ancient architecture, chiseled out by wind and tide and so nearly conforming to human art, is, to say the least, a matter of wonder. And then to view along a line of nearly seven hundred miles unrivaled mountain and valley scenery, to watch the fantastic phases of earth and sky, ride through gorgeous cañons, survey dizzy heights and lofty pinnacles and study the walls and bastions and battlements, where

> "Huge piers and frowning forms of gods sustain
> The everlasting arches, dark and wide—"

this, indeed, is employment fit for the gods themselves. The spell of these enchantments may be gradually broken but the impressions made are not to be effaced. Such an experience carries with it more than momentary excitement, more than the ephemeral entertainment of the short journey, furnishing, as it does, both matter and inspiration for thought and study. The whole phenomenon is an open volume

GATEWAY TO THE GARDEN OF THE GODS.

"Telling of time in the primeval morn
    When beast and man yet slumbered in the ground,
    When sentient life lay in the dust unborn,
    And wind and wave rolled on in ceaseless round;

"Of ancient epochs and of glaciers gone,
    Of rocks, abraded as the ages waned,
    Of times when earth became a floral lawn,
    And all the chiselings through cycles gained."

There is, too, the moral, as well as the reflective phase, since these revelations of the rocks can not but awaken a solemn awe and emotions of reverence. They teach the littleness and weakness of man, the folly of his finery and the poverty of his pomp and splendor. Such grand exhibitions of nature also widen the field of vision and give broader conceptions of the world. They enlarge the mental horizon and with it the view of life. Trifles and petty annoyances, which make up the average lot of misery, are unprivileged intruders in the royal presence of these sublimer thoughts.

www.ingramcontent.com/pod-product-compliance
Lightning Source LLC
Chambersburg PA
CBHW032108220426
43664CB00008B/1180